BLOOMING

BLOOMING

FINDING GIFTS IN THE SHIT OF LIFE

CARRINGTON SMITH

LIONCREST
PUBLISHING

BLOOMING

Finding Gifts in the Shit of Life

ISBN 978-1-5445-2380-4 *Hardcover*
   978-1-5445-2378-1 *Paperback*
   978-1-5445-2379-8 *Ebook*
   978-1-5445-2381-1 *Audiobook*

For my mother,
who told me I was braver
than she was.

For Stephanie Woodard,
because I'm still here.

For my boys:
you taught me how to love
unconditionally.

And for those of you fighting
to love yourself:
I am you.

CONTENTS

CHAPTER NINETEEN

BLOOMING

AUTHOR'S NOTE

*"You own everything that happened to you.
Tell your stories. If people wanted you to write warmly
about them, they should have behaved better."*

—ANNE LAMOTT

These are my stories. I share them to the best of my recollection. Others may remember or perceive them differently, for we each bring our own perceptions, mindsets, and filters to every memory. My purpose in writing this book is to discover the gifts in life, not to call out people or hurt anyone. With that in mind, I've changed the names and identifying details of many of the people in this book. Dialogue may not be exact, but it reflects the substance of a conversation as I recall it. Each of these stories describes a moment in time and not the entirety of a person, so I ask that the reader not damn an individual for a moment in time when he or she behaved badly. We all behave badly from time to time, myself included. I choose to forgive those who caused me pain. And I hope that they will do the same.

WHY I WROTE THIS BOOK

*"Memoir is about handing over your life
to someone and saying, this is what I went through,
this is who I am, and maybe you can
learn something from it."*

—JEANNETTE WALLS

This book was birthed during the pandemic. During the shit-storm of a lifetime, I felt compelled to share how life has taught me to view times like these as full of growth and opportunity. You see, shit is quite literally fertilizer. It provides the nutrients needed for life to flourish and grow. It is in life's messes, the failures, the difficulties—the shit—that we find what we need to grow and bloom into our greatness.

As I write, millions of people have lost their jobs because of the pandemic. Hundreds of thousands have lost their lives. Everywhere people are struggling with the existential questions: Do I matter? Without a job, what do I base my self-worth on? If I die tomorrow, what will I be remembered for?

Over the twenty years of my career as an executive search professional, I've interviewed thousands of candidates. I've been blessed with an incredible track record. Most candidates stay in their jobs for years and regularly get promoted. What's the secret sauce? I focus on character and values. My favorite question to ask to understand who someone is and what they value is: "We all have moments that define us; can you tell me about a moment that shaped you and how?"

The answers to this question tell me more about a candidate than almost any other. Based on their answers, I discover things like emotional resilience, authenticity, grit, courage, empathy, persistence, wisdom, creativity, integrity, curiosity, passion, self-discipline, perseverance, resourcefulness, reframing, hope, leadership, collaboration, positive attitude, strategic thinking, and problem-solving.

For years, I've lived in fear that someone would turn the question around on me. How would I answer? There have been so many defining moments—many of them raw and ugly. But, after decades of prying into the lives of others, I needed to uncover the answer for myself. Life-altering events, like a once-in-a-lifetime pandemic, have a way of pushing you to face those deep truths. This book is my answer to that question.

Thank you to the individuals who have trusted me with their stories. I honor you and your courage to share them with me. To those of you pondering these existential questions, it is my hope that through sharing my story, it will help you to discover your gifts in the shit of life.

CHAPTER ONE

FINDING MY VOICE

*"Owning our story and loving ourselves
through that process is the bravest
thing that we will ever do."*

—BRENÉ BROWN

It was an October night in 1986. He had been raping me for hours. He left the room to take a break, locking me inside. I did my best to redress myself, but the buttons had been ripped from my shirt. I pulled it tight around me and climbed the ladder to the upper bunk bed. Moving to the farthest corner, I pulled my knees in, wrapping my arms around them and pressing them into my chest. I wanted to disappear. My body hurt. I felt numb—except for the tears I could feel running down my face. The bunk bed was up against a window, giving me a view of the night sky and the yard two stories below. I knew he would come back eventually, and pondered leaping out of the window. I would likely break some bones, but it would be a relief from this. As I considered this option, I heard the door unlock. Fear ran through my body like ice. I felt my pulse quicken.

"I'm not done with you yet," he said. He must have taken something while he was out of the room. His eyes were crazy. He looked hungry—for me. I pushed myself farther back into the corner, pulling my knees in closer, trying to disappear completely. He climbed the ladder, picked me up, and carried me down. He ripped my clothes off again. I felt myself tear as he took his pleasure without lubrication. As he penetrated me again and again, I left my body. I dissociated. Later, I learned this was the body's way of protecting itself during trauma.

A few hours later, he was done. He handed me my clothes and told me I could go. He watched me as I dressed myself. I had large, angry rug burns on the tops of my feet, lower back, and elbows. I left his room and heard him close the door behind me, then lock it. I crept down the hallway to the massive central staircase, hugging the wall as I held my shirt closed. It was dark in the house now and everyone was in bed. I opened the massive front door and stepped into the night. I remember the walk home to my sorority house feeling cold and painful. It hurt to walk. I let myself into the sorority house, quietly climbing the stairs to my room. I stripped naked and made my way to the shower room. Everyone was asleep so I had the shower to myself. I stood under the shower, wincing from pain as the water hit torn skin. I put my pj's on and found a daybed to curl up on. I didn't want to risk waking anyone, so I didn't go into the sleeping dorm (a large room full of bunk beds where all the girls slept). I lay there in the fetal position, tears running down my face, not sure how to comprehend what just happened. My body was in shock. I didn't sleep. I couldn't.

The next morning, I sought out a sorority sister, Courtney, for advice. I was terrified of getting pregnant and I was terrified someone would find out what had happened to me. You see, two years prior, another girl in a campus sorority, Abigail, had been gang-raped at another fraternity. When she told her story, no one believed her. Instead, she was vilified. She was labeled a slut and got kicked out of her sorority at Washington State University.

I confided in Courtney what had happened. The Tri Deltas and Sigma Nus were doing homecoming together. At WSU, homecoming was a massive celebration. Sororities paired off with fraternities to design and build yard decorations. The best ones won a prize and bragging rights. We participated in our own version of Olympic-type games and attended a series of parties leading up to the big football game. One afternoon, I went over to the Sigma Nu house with a group of Tri Delts to work on the yard decorations. I met a boy I'll call Gregory when I arrived. After working outside for a couple of hours, a few of my sorority sisters and I were invited inside to have a beer. The keg was upstairs, so we climbed the massive wood staircase to the second floor. I was handed a cup of beer and Gregory pulled me into his room. The next thing I remember is the thunderous sound of his door being kicked open. We had an audience now. I could hear shouts and catcalls from a group of guys jostling to see in the room. I realized that I was naked, and that Gregory was on top of me, inside of me. I tried to hide my face. Gregory pulled himself off me, yelling at his fraternity brothers to "get the fuck out." The door had multiple dead bolts, some which required keys. He locked them all before returning to me. He had raped me for hours, leaving that one time and returning to rape me again. I shared all of this with Courtney. She scrunched up her nose at me. "Are you sure you didn't want him to have sex with you?" I tried again to explain to her that this wasn't consensual sex. This was rape. But Abigail's legacy weighed on her. "Just be really sure," she warned. "Be careful how you handle this—remember what happened to Abigail." I felt myself descend into darkness. She hadn't provided the support that I had hoped for. I was on my own.

I wandered down to the Student Health Center and had them examine me. Observing my torn skin, rug burns, and bruises, the doctor asked me if there was anything I wanted to tell him. I was afraid he would report it to the police, and I would end up like Abigail. So, instead of telling him the truth, I insisted it was just rough sex. I had recently watched a Phil Donahue show where they had discussed a medical breakthrough which they were calling the "morning after pill," and I asked the doctor if he had heard of it. I didn't know much about it except that it was intended to be taken shortly after intercourse to prevent pregnancy when no contraception had been used. Pregnancy was my biggest concern. My parents were vehemently pro-life. So much so that I was forced to watch graphic videos of actual abortions, including ultrasound views of different types of abortions as they occurred, and the disposal of the fetuses. Their version of a family movie night. Lucky for me, the doctor at the Student Health Center was familiar. While he didn't have the actual "morning after pill" because it had not yet been approved by the FDA (it wasn't until 2001—I was very lucky to have seen that Donahue episode), the doctor said that it was essentially the equivalent of taking about eight birth control pills all at once. The idea was to push your estrogen level way up and then drop it, causing a period. He said that this was such new science that he had no idea if it could cause cancer or what the adverse reactions might be, other than that it would probably cause nausea. I took the eight birth control pills and swallowed them all at once. It wasn't long before I was puking nonstop.

The following day, the Tri Delts were invited to a mixer with the Sigma Nus at their house. I had been walking around like a zombie, going through the motions of sorority life. As afraid as I was of seeing Gregory again, I was equally afraid that someone would find out what happened to me, and I would get kicked out of my sorority. I was desperate to fit in and didn't want to draw attention to myself by staying behind, so I went with about seventy girls to the Sigma Nu house. The party was in the basement, and as I rounded the corner to enter the room where the party was being held, Gregory was leaning against the wall waiting for me. I stopped cold. I was frozen. He approached me and grabbed my hand. Opening it, he placed my earrings into my hand. Bent and broken, they must have come off during the rape. Stepping back, with his eyes looking at the floor, he said, "I'm sorry. I'm really sorry." Those words saved my life. He knew what he had done.

I escaped from the party back to the sorority house as soon as I could. Lying awake in the sleeping dorm, tears flowing freely, I tried to process all that had happened.

The numbness overwhelmed me. Unable to speak to anyone about what had happened, I felt myself slip into darkness. I stopped going to class. I started sleeping all the time. I wasn't bathing. I started calling home and begging them to let me come home. The cost of a flight at that time was fifty dollars. My parents told me that they couldn't afford it and that I would have to wait until

Thanksgiving to come home. Didn't they understand? I was so depressed, I was contemplating suicide. My life wasn't worth fifty dollars? My father insisted that they couldn't afford it and I would have to wait. My depression became so severe, I was called in front of our chapter's "Standards Board." This was a group of the chapter's officers who dealt with people who broke the rules or hurt the sorority's reputation. The Standards Board informed me that I was "getting everyone down," and that I needed "to stop being so depressed" and should "work on being happier." I was devastated. Their "intervention" had the exact opposite effect. They communicated that it was more important to *appear* happy than to deal with the underlying problem. This only made me more depressed.

Somehow, I survived the period from mid-October to Thanksgiving break—I was in a steady decline and an ever-deepening depression. As was our usual form, three of my pledge sisters and I piled into my Honda Civic sedan and headed west from Pullman on Highway 26 toward Seattle. The highway was crowded with all the other kids headed home for break, so we set out early to avoid heavy traffic. The weather wasn't good, so we took note when we saw four Sigma Phi Epsilons speed past us. One of the girls in my car, Kathy, was dating a Sig Ep. She recognized some of the boys, waving at them as they passed. We were rocking out to ABC's "Look of Love" when we began to notice things askew across the highway. Papers were flying by, and then we saw a typewriter in the road. As the Sig Ep's sedan came into view, Kathy started to scream. I turned off the music and slowed the car to a creep. Their car was on the wrong side of the road. There were shards of glass and car parts everywhere. The rear driver's side door was open, and books and papers were strewn across the highway. As we got closer, we could see the driver's body ejected through the windshield and lying on the hood. Another body was lying outside the car, and a head was partially protruding from the smashed-out rear passenger window. There were several cars stopped, and people were running to and fro. "We need to stop and help," I said. "No," Kathy screamed, "I can't look! I can't look! I know him!!" Sonya and Allison argued that there were other people stopped. I hesitated. Scanning the bloody scene, I knew almost everyone was dead. "Ok, we will go call for help," I acquiesced. (This being before cell phones, calling for help was as important as stopping.) As we drove off, we passed an ambulance headed in their direction about ten miles down the road.

Snow began to fall with increasing intensity as we got closer to Snoqualmie Pass. We were all sobbing and shaking, but we had to get through the mountain pass to get home. My nerves were fried. The roads were unsafe. I wanted to find a place to stop. The girls all just wanted to get home. A chorus of voices commanded that I keep driving. The snow was so thick that I could barely see; a blanket of fluffy white flakes obscured the road from view. The road now matched the surrounding landscape, and we could no longer see where the road and the sky separated. We were experiencing a total whiteout.

We were in the mountain pass now, but the road had become undrivable. We had to stop to put chains on my tires. Four sorority girls trying to put chains on tires in a snowstorm. How many sorority girls did it take? Zero. After about twenty minutes of total confusion, tears, swearing, and frustration, a massive Snowcat with stadium-sized overhead lights appeared on the horizon. Like an angel sent from heaven, a state trooper appeared. He informed us that they had closed the mountain pass behind us. We were the last car through. The trooper put our chains on in minutes and followed us down the mountain. His massive overhead lights broke through the whiteness and made my stomach drop. We had no idea how close we had been to driving over the edge of the mountain. His lights illuminated cars and semitrucks that had tumbled over the edge and were now getting covered in snow. God was watching out for us. We were the lucky ones. We reached the bottom of the mountain and waved goodbye with sincere gratitude.

We had reached Issaquah, where Sonya lived. I was incapable of driving anymore. It was all too much. I crashed at her house but slept fitfully. I felt like I was slipping on ice…and blood. I would wake up to my legs kicking out, slipping on the sheets. I was spinning, crashing into cars, falling off the mountain. Bodies flying. Papers flying. The typewriter in the road. The body on the hood of the car.

The next morning, we anxiously reached for a newspaper to glean any details from the crash. The four Sig Eps in the sedan were passing and hit another car heading in the opposite direction head-on. Two of the four Sig Eps and the driver of the other car died instantly. A third Sig Ep died en route to the hospital. One Sig Ep survived. I hugged my friends tightly and drove the rest of the way home. I was incredibly shaken, numb, and traumatized by all that transpired over the previous few days and months. So, when I finally arrived home, I was happy to see my parents and get a hug from my mother.

I crawled into bed. Emotionally worn out, I couldn't stop crying. It was all too much—the rape, the lack of support, the car accident. I would fall asleep and jerk awake. My face would be wet with tears. I felt, like my car, my life was spinning out of control. My mother came in to check on me. It was dark now; night had fallen. I lay in my old antique four-poster bed, the same one from my childhood. I pulled the ancient bed linens to my neck. My mother sat at the foot of the bed, expressing concern over my emotional state. "Now, what is this all about? Why all this *DRAMA* about wanting to kill yourself? Why all the tears? Where has this behavior come from?" my mom inquired. I took a deep breath. My mother had served as the executive director of the Everett Crisis Pregnancy Center. She had told me stories about classmates of mine visiting the center. They were people I knew who had turned to drugs or become strippers and then shown up pregnant. She had counseled all of these people on their options other than abortion. I hoped that she would be there for me as she had been for my classmates. "Mom, I was raped," I said through sobs. Before I could continue, she stood up, her face red and angry. In a clipped voice, she said, "I am so disappointed in you. We had hoped that you would remain a virgin until you were married." I was so taken aback by her response. My mouth was wide open, my jaw hanging in dismay. "You must *NEVER* speak of this again, and you must *NEVER* tell your father!" she commanded. I shook my head in fearful assent. If this was her reaction, Lord only knew what he would do if he found out. I hung my head in shame. I told her that I needed some money for a medical issue. I was worried. My mother, exasperated, said, "I will give you some money in the morning, but you are on your own." She stormed out of the room. I felt so alone and ashamed.

I nestled in my bed, contemplating my recent experiences. I felt untethered. Homeless. Alone. Maybe it was because I looked death in the face the day before and saw close-up the ripple effects of losing someone, but suddenly I didn't want to die. I also knew that I didn't want the rape to define me. I had the radio on, and Madonna's song "Live to Tell" was playing. I turned the volume up and reflected on her lyrics. In that moment, I resolved that keeping the rape a secret wouldn't kill me. I just needed to formulate a plan to get past it. I needed to get the fuck out of Dodge. Get the hell out of this crazy town. I needed a fresh start.

The next morning, I sprung it on my parents. I wanted to transfer to a different school. My brother was graduating from Stanford, and I had gone to a state school to help pay for his school. It was my turn. I think the fact that they saw my mood brighten helped my cause. My mother thought it was a great idea. It was early enough. There was still plenty of time to apply. My sorority little sister, Margie, had just returned from visiting the University of Texas at Austin and could not stop raving about it. Good school, warm climate, no snow. Perfect—I was sold. I didn't know a soul there. I wouldn't deal with the rape. I wouldn't talk about it. I would do as I was told. I felt a sense of hope for the first time in weeks. Something to look forward to. A clean slate. A fresh start. Far away. No snow. No rapist.

I transferred to the University of Texas at Austin, and I tried to forget about the rape. I didn't want that event to define me. I honored my mother's wish and kept the rape a secret. What I didn't realize was that by not talking about it, it was owning me. I suffered from poor self-esteem and became promiscuous. My rapist sent me the message that I wasn't worthy of being treated well; I was only worthy of meaningless sex. I kept reliving this experience. I was incapable of forming any meaningful relationships.

Then, in law school, I met Rob. We became close friends and eventually started sleeping together. Because we had been friends first, the experience felt different. He valued me as a person. As we got closer, I panicked and suddenly lashed out, causing drama to push him away. I broke down. It had been six years since the rape, and, keeping the promise to my mother, I had never spoken about it. I felt that I owed Rob an explanation for my bizarre behavior. I sat down at my computer, and the story poured out of me. The first story that I had ever written about my life. Somehow writing about the rape was easier than talking about it. It felt safer. I found my voice. I could express myself freely through writing without the immediate feedback of someone's biases or judgments. I printed it out and left it in his folder at law school (we didn't have email yet), terrified of what he might think. His response surprised me. He was the first person to handle my rape with compassion. He embraced and accepted me. This was a monumental moment for me. I began to look at myself through a different, kinder lens. I sought out therapy.

Years later, after my second divorce, I was dating a much younger guy. There were still things that might happen in bed that could cause me to go cold or react violently (you put your hand on my throat, and I will punch you). I was trying to explain, so I shared my story of being raped in college. When I finished, he said, "Well, I have zero sympathy for you. You should have known better. Everyone knows about date rape. It's all over the internet!" I wasn't telling him my story to garner sympathy but, rather, to help him understand why I reacted the way that I did sometimes. I shook my head in dismay at his callous response. "First," I told him, "there was no internet when this happened. Second, we didn't even have personal computers yet. Third, we didn't even have Oprah yet. Fourth, this wasn't date rape. There was no date.

This was a predator preying on an unsuspecting victim. Fifth, I didn't ask to be raped. Sixth, we are done." I shook my head in disgust as he sat there in stunned silence, trying to conceive of a world without the internet.

I had been told to shut up and not tell my story. It makes people feel uncomfortable. But the truth is that my power, my secret weapons, my gifts are IN my stories; that is where I discovered the authentic me—where I discovered the gifts, the buried treasure, in all the shit. It is in the debris of life, in the fire, that I found out who I was and what I was made of.

As I was writing this book, I stumbled across Augusten Burroughs's book *This Is How*. In it, he wrote:

> What does help the person who has been raped is to chew it up and then spit it the hell out. And by chew it up I mean talk about it, write about it, paint it, make a movie about it, and then be done with it and move on. Because here's the truth about rape: you do not have to be victimized by it forever. You can take this awful, bottomless horror the rapist has inflicted on you, and you can seize it and recycle it into something wonderful and helpful and useful. You can, in this way, transform what was "done" to you into something that was "given" to you in the form of brutally raw material. You can, in other words, accept this hideous thing and embrace it and take complete control of the experience and reshape it as you please. This is not to deny the experience and how devastating it is; it is to accept the experience on the deepest level as your own possession now. An experience that is now part of you. Instead of allowing it to be a tap that drains you, you can force it into duty in service to your creative or intellectual goals.

He was so right. I had just lived this experience.

The rape, as horrible as it was, taught me that I was a survivor. I was not a victim; I was victimized. There is a massive difference. How I viewed that event—the story that I told myself—was critical to my survival. I learned the power of perspective. I was not a victim. I was victim*ized*. And in turn, I *survived*. I was a survivor. There is power in being tested and surviving. It's called emotional resilience. I learned that I could navigate the most difficult circumstances. This, in turn, bred a quiet confidence.

In 1997, I turned on the *Oprah Winfrey Show* and the guest for that day was Gavin de Becker. They were talking about his most recent book, *The Gift of Fear: Survival Signals That Protect Us from Violence*. I sat mesmerized listening to them talk and then rushed out to Barnes & Noble to buy the book. It is a book that I have read countless times and recommend to people on a regular basis.

In his book, de Becker begins with a client, Kelly, describing her rape. By sharing her story, "Kelly is about to learn that listening to one small survival signal saved her life, just as failing to follow so many others had put her at risk in the first place." In her story, her subconscious recognized that her rapist's act of closing a window was incongruous with what he was telling her—that he would leave. De Becker notes, "Since he was dressed and supposedly leaving, he had no other reason to close her window. It was that subtle signal that warned her, but it was fear that gave her the courage to get up without hesitation and follow close behind the man who intended to kill her." By unearthing this, Kelly "felt a new confidence in herself, knowing she had acted on that signal, knowing she had saved her own life."

De Becker wrote his book based on the belief that there is a "universal code of violence" and that by teaching people the signals, they can avoid becoming victims. How did de Becker become an expert in this field? He grew up in a household so violent that he learned to recognize the clues. "Pre-incident indicators are those detectable factors that occur before the outcome being predicted. Stepping on the first rung of a ladder is a significant pre-incident indicator to reaching the top; stepping on the sixth even more so. Since everything a person does is created twice—once in the mind and once in its execution—ideas and impulses are pre-incident indicators for action. The woman's threats to kill revealed an idea that was one step toward the outcome; her introduction of the gun into the argument with her husband was another, as was its purchase some months earlier."

Before de Becker was thirteen, he "saw a man shot, saw another beaten and kicked to unconsciousness, saw a friend struck near lethally in the face and head with a steel rod, saw his mother become a heroin addict, saw his sister beaten, and himself was a veteran of beatings." He learned to make high-stakes predictions to survive. With such a horrible childhood, de Becker could have grown up to become a criminal. Instead, he used his gift—the ability to predict violence—to propel him into a career advising presidents, celebrities, and other VIPs. By owning his story—instead of it owning him—he was able to recognize and capitalize on his gift.

As Brené Brown said in *The Gifts of Imperfection*: "Owning our story can be hard but not nearly as difficult as spending our lives running from it. Embracing our vulnerabilities is risky but not nearly as dangerous as giving up on love and belonging and joy—the experiences that make us the most vulnerable. Only when we are brave enough to explore the darkness will we discover the infinite power of our light."

The reason that I gravitated to de Becker's book was not so much because of the rape—it was his personal story and how he claimed it and used it to propel him through life. Instead of pretending he had a great childhood, he owned his story. He fully embraced it. He explored his darkness, and by recognizing what he had gained from his horrific childhood, found his light. He made his story *serve him* and catapult him to greatness. By owning his story, he has gifted us with the lessons and wisdom he received from it.

Following the wisdom of Brown and de Becker, I'm owning my story. Every gritty, shitty, brutal, ugly aspect of it. I embrace love, belonging, and joy. This little light of mine, I'm gonna let it shine.

CHAPTER TWO

FAMILY LEGACY

"Family dysfunction rolls down from generation to generation, like a fire in the woods, taking down everything in its path, until one person in one generation has the courage to turn and face the flames. That person brings peace to their ancestors and spares the children that follow."

—TERRY REAL

To understand my story, we have to travel back a few generations, for my family legacy has cast a shadow on much of my life. On my mother's side, my great-great-grandfather, Albrecht Pagenstecher, was the founder of International Paper Company. Traded on the New York Stock Exchange, it is the largest pulp and paper company in the world. One of the most influential businessmen of his time, he rose literally from rags to riches: Albrecht and his two brothers acquired the patent to make paper out of wood pulp instead of rags as it previously had been made. They lived an incredible life, building and selling numerous companies. They socialized with the Astors, Vanderbilts, and DuPonts. Indeed, Commodore Vanderbilt gave a home to one of my relatives as a wedding gift. My mother's family was one of the early families in the venerable *Social Register*. Her grandfather, Albrecht Pagenstecher, Jr., known as Odie, served as the president of the Manufacturers Paper Company, and on the board of directors of Garfield National Bank, which merged with Chase Manhattan Bank. He served on the board of trustees of the Storm King School in Cornwall, New York. In 1905, Odie built a twenty-room mansion in Cornwall on the Hudson which he called "Upyonda" at the end of a mile-long driveway. My mother would tell us stories and show us black-and-white silent movies of Upyonda, their residence on Fifth Avenue, and their summer home in Middlebury, Vermont. One of the lucky few to own automobiles at the turn of the century, Odie had a chauffeur, gardener, butler, chef, maids, and other servants.

My maternal grandmother, Mimi, attended Miss Porter's School in Farmington, Connecticut. Upon graduation, she was sent to finishing school in Switzerland. Then, she had her debut at the Ritz-Carlton in New York City in 1932.

The expectations were that Mimi would marry well and continue her lifestyle as a socialite, playing sports, entertaining, and engaging in philanthropic endeavors. She joined the New York City Junior League and regularly played tennis at Piping Rock Club. In 1938, she married Charles Augustus Frank, Jr. ("Charlie") at the chapel of the Fifth Avenue Presbyterian Church in Manhattan. Her parents were excited about this partnership. My grandfather was sweet and kind, and a great social match. He was raised in a mansion called "Charlon House" that was commissioned by his father in Glen Cove, New York, on Long Island's famed Gold Coast, a cluster of townships on the North Shore of Long Island that once was home to the greatest concentration of wealth and power in North America and served as the subject matter for F. Scott Fitzgerald's *The Great Gatsby* and Nelson DeMille's eponymous novel. His father, Charles, Sr., founded Gotham National Bank, which merged with Manufacturers Trust Company and a brokerage firm, Charles A. Frank & Co., that earned him a seat on the New York Stock Exchange. He maintained that seat for thirty-eight years and became known as the "Dean of Wall Street."

No doubt, they were living at the top of society. But this is where things get fuzzy. Families like to share the good stories, but not the bad. In 1955, Upyonda burned to the ground in a spectacular fire visible for miles. The land was later donated to the community and is now known as Pagenstecher Park. I've heard a variety of stories about what happened with Odie: he had a nervous breakdown; he went to Germany for a few months to take a break and while he was gone, his brothers took control of his business; he was forced to resign from the board of directors. I don't know that I'll ever know the truth. In all likelihood, like other families of European descent during that time, they followed the practice of male-preference primogeniture, the right by law or custom of the first-born male legitimate child to inherit the parents' entire or main estate. Mimi, being the youngest and a female, may have needed to marry well to maintain her lifestyle. It is unclear what happened with Charles, Sr. One story was that he had an affair and ran off with his mistress, but that doesn't explain where the money went.

In the end, my maternal grandfather and grandmother were two very spoiled children who were brought up expecting to live a life of leisure funded by family money. Yet, for some reason that remains a mystery to me, the money did not pass to either of them. They were suddenly faced with maintaining a lifestyle that their finances did not support, especially with four children. My mother was the oldest, followed by Charles III, then Gerry, and Helen.

As they scrambled to make ends meet, their concern and focus were on maintaining social status. They insisted that their children attend the same schools—for my grandfather, that meant the boys would attend the Hill School and Yale. My grandfather maintained his interest in polo and sailing, and while a great father, never amounted to much professionally. My grandmother was bitter and resentful. After a decadent child- and young-adulthood, she suddenly lacked the funds to keep up with her high-society friends. Instead, she devoted her attention to imposing her expectations for what amounted to a successful life on her children and grandchildren. She put a premium on athletic ability, going to the right schools, maintaining memberships in the right clubs, and marrying well.

On my father's side, our roots go back to the Revolutionary War. My father's sister was active in the Daughters of the American Revolution and the Colonial Dames. My paternal grandfather invented the hydraulic lift that is used to repair automobiles. He was the CEO of a company that sold lifts, brakes, and other automobile-related items. My grandmother, whom we called Bahma, was one of the first female newspaper reporters in New York City, writing society and advice columns. She was vibrant and sassy. They had two children—my father and his older sister, Debbie. A career woman first, my grandmother did not have my father until age forty. My father does not speak about his childhood. At all. Ever. What I learned about my father's childhood, I learned from his sister. He contracted polio at age five and was critically ill. While he recovered, his parents hired a man to carry him around. His sister, a psychologist, suggested that his interactions with this man may explain why he developed a deep hatred for homosexuals. In any event, he was left with a permanent limp, and a desperate need to control the world around him.

My mother also attended Miss Porter's School, then Vassar, where she took acting alongside Jane Fonda. She loved to tell us stories about those years. She was vibrant and fun then. She took a job at the University of Pennsylvania Medical School because she wanted to marry a doctor. That is where she met my father. They were married in June 1962 in Glen Cove, Long Island.

In 1966, my maternal grandfather fell down the stairs and broke his hip. He died shortly thereafter. My mother was heartbroken and never fully recovered from this. She loved her father deeply and missed him greatly.

In 1967, my paternal grandfather died following a car accident. Again, I don't know the circumstances, but according to his sister, my father was cut out of his father's will and removed from his life insurance policy.

All of this happened before I was born, yet each of these facts has shaped who I am. I was born into a family with high expectations, wrapped up in who they used to be, clinging to social status, and full of resentment. It was a family short on love, compassion, and support. A family where children were seen but not heard. My family embraced the Protestant work ethic—"Pull yourself up by your bootstraps"—to the extreme degree that we were more a collection of people competing for resources, attention, accolades, and love, than a family looking out for one another. I was supposed to live up to the lofty expectations of my family, but I was on my own to meet them.

Growing up, I was regularly told how our family was different, special, more important, better than, more accomplished and successful than other families. This "grand delusion" was central to how my parents operated. My mother fueled this narrative by insisting that we know how to curtsy, have proper posture (making us walk around the house with books on our heads), and have impeccable manners in case we were ever invited to have tea with the Queen of England. Apparently, somewhere on the Smith side of the family, we are (very) distant relatives of the royal family. So, my parents insisted that this was a real possibility and that we should be prepared. I'm still waiting for my invitation.

My mother, like her mother, prepared me to be a great wife. I was expected to marry well. I was trained by my parents to be dependent. I was to look to my parents for everything. Yet, I saw how miserable my mother and maternal grandmother were. I could only conclude that dependency bred depression and resentment. The only genuinely happy family member I knew was my paternal grandmother, who lived to 105. A successful journalist and career woman before marrying, she never gave up her independence. She was a trendsetter, an original. The twin conflicts of *wife versus career woman* and *conforming versus expression* haunted me for much of my life.

As the youngest of three children, my parents did not place much confidence in my future, all the focus and investment being on my older brother and sister. It was as if I had been dismissed. I was an afterthought—the recipient of leftovers and hand-me-downs. I was still expected to live up to the lofty expectations of my family, but I was the horse that they weren't betting on or investing in. This lack of confidence in me is what propelled me to academic and professional success. Like Glenn Close in *Fatal Attraction*, I was crying out, "I won't be ignored!"

CHAPTER THREE

DADDY ISSUES

> *"I cannot think of any need in childhood as strong*
> *as the need for a father's protection."*
>
> **—SIGMUND FREUD**

At age three, I was tiny in stature with porcelain skin and a smattering of freckles across my face. I had huge green eyes and straight strawberry-blonde hair cut variously in pageboy and pixie cuts. The youngest of three children, I was born eighteen months after my sister, Tiffany, the middle child. She had blue eyes and long, naturally curly red hair that I envied, and the personality that went with it. Tiffany was often the center of attention. She was much taller than I, as was my brother, Todd. I truly was the runt of the litter. Todd, who was eighteen months older than Tiffany, had wavy, dark brown hair and brown eyes. He could have resembled a slightly less handsome young Tom Cruise except for the black horn-rimmed glasses, Sears Toughskins, and striped shirts my mother always made him wear.

The year was 1971. We lived in a rented guest cottage on a sprawling farm off Evergreen Road in Oxford, Maryland. Our backyard ended at the Chesapeake Bay, where my father docked his three sailboats. One summer evening, we sailed into town for dinner. There was no space at the pier for us to dock, so my father anchored our boat, and we used a dinghy to get to shore. As dinner was ending, the sky grew dark, and the water became choppy. My mother grew nervous. "John, there's a thunderstorm coming; let's get a ride back to the house and come back for the boat later." My father was more worried about his sailboat. "Dottie, I need to get back out there and drop a second anchor. The boat isn't properly moored to withstand a storm! Now, get into the dinghy!" my father replied tersely. We climbed into our dinghy, and as we left the shore, the sky became black, the sea whipped up, and lightning exploded in the sky. The sky opened and rain pelted us. The dinghy began to fill with water as lightning chased us. We were in the vortex of a storm. My sister, brother, and I screamed in terror as my father rowed us back to the boat. We climbed into our sailboat, the Morning Star, as lightning pierced the water where we had just been. We flung our bodies down the stairs to the relative safety below. As the boat tilted and rocked, thunder sounded, lightning crackled, and my mother unleashed her fury on my father. "What the hell were you thinking? You nearly got us all killed! Your damn boat is not more important than our lives! And when are you going to tell me the truth about Judy? Why would your secretary just up and leave without any notice? I mean it, John. I want the truth and things need to change!" my mother screamed at my father.

Six months later, we departed for the small town of Everett, Washington (population 50,000 at the time). The journey began suddenly and with a huge jolt, much like the long, rough train ride we endured across the country to get there. The train departed from Baltimore, Maryland, where my father had started his medical practice after completing a fellowship at Johns Hopkins University. My parents were both born on Long Island and had attended schools on the East Coast. All of our family and friends resided on the East Coast. Yet, we boarded a train for this mysterious place where my father had purchased a house for us, without input from our mother, and not knowing a soul. My mother complained frequently. She was devastated to be leaving her family and friends behind. As the train left Baltimore, we left behind whispers of why my father's secretary had disappeared. The farther we traveled, the whispers faded until we could no longer hear them.

We arrived in Everett, a mostly industrial seaside town, and my father took a job at a local clinic and as the head of the intensive care unit at a local hospital. Our new home was on a beautiful lot overlooking Puget Sound. The views were breathtaking. On a clear day, we could see the Cascade and Olympic Mountains. In the summertime, we luxuriated in breathtaking sunsets and listened to the seals yelp below. But always we lived in the shadow of the nearby paper mills—a constant, cruel reminder of our family's storied past—and on any given day, the wind might shift and cast a sour smell our way.

Our home was surrounded by an enormous front and back yard. In the center of the backyard was a stone birdbath with a flower garden. The backyard ended abruptly with a cliff dropping off more than 200 feet. Below us ran railroad tracks and the road to the Everett Yacht Club. On either side of our backyard, we had enormous rhododendron bushes and apple trees that provided a regular stream of fruit.

Me with my brother and sister in the backyard of our home in Everett, Washington.

The house itself wasn't huge. There were two bedrooms and one bath upstairs and one bedroom and one bath downstairs. My parents took the downstairs bedroom. My sister and I shared a bedroom, and my brother had his own room. My parents collected many antiques from our days on the East Coast and filled our house to the brim with them. We had three grandfather clocks that would gong on the hour. We had many chests of drawers and a dining room table that must have been something special because it was warped. Tiffany and I each slept in a queen-size four-poster bed—on wheels. We had hardwood floors in our bedroom, so there were nights when I would wake up and my bed would have moved. I was never sure if it was because of the train below or an earthquake, which were also common. Our mother made our beds up out of the old sheets and scratchy wool blankets that she kept in a massive wood trunk. She wallpapered the upstairs bathroom with paper that had ABCs on it as if we were babies. We were each bought one set of towels, which were never replaced. I used that same set of towels for thirteen years until they disintegrated. About five years after we moved to Everett, my father decided that we needed to add onto our house. A master bedroom, bathroom, and study were added upstairs, and a large family room with cathedral ceilings and a second dining room were added downstairs. The new addition was modern and was in sharp contrast to the traditional main house. The new addition had exposed beams in the family room, parquet floors, and shag carpet. My parents ran out of money while building. The result was a mismatched master bath with cheap tile and wallpaper. The lack of cohesion in the house was jarring, much like our family life.

Growing up, there were always lots of secrets. Tension was thick in our house. Every one of us was terrified of my father. His moods were dark and his temper short. He never smiled. Instead, he had a permanent scowl on his face. Running an intensive care unit increased my father's stress—the harder the cases he had to deal with, the harder he was on us. He let us know that everything at home needed to be about him so that he could relax. We all tip-toed around him and tried to make sure everything was just how he wanted it, but he was like a bomb that could go off at any moment.

I did what I could to help out. Since he was in charge of the ICU, we had nurses calling our house all the time. From the age of four, he had me trained to screen the nurses' calls. He was always complaining about them and saying most of them were idiots. He taught me to relay their questions to him and to act sassy and annoyed. To all the nurses out there, I'm sorry. I appreciate you and the hard work that you do.

My father also worked as a pulmonologist at a local clinic. It didn't last long though. We were told that he left after being accused of "laying his hands on a patient and praying for them." I wondered if these two things had happened at the same time. Whatever the reason, the steady paycheck was gone.

My father had graduated from and been trained at two of the most prestigious medical schools in the world. He should have been highly recruited for top opportunities in major cities. But instead of being sought after, he was struggling in his career. Eventually, he opened his own practice, but his income was always unpredictable. There were good times and lean times and this led to constant fights between my parents about money.

One of the patients at his new practice was a man of American Indian descent from a nearby reservation. After we added onto the house, my parents' old bedroom on the main floor became the temporary home for a variety of guests, including this man's wife and daughter, Inez and Irena. They lived with us for about a month as he recovered in the hospital. After they left, they could not afford to pay my father's bills, so they gave us a side of beef as compensation. I'm not sure the age of this cow, but based on the toughness of the meat, I would guess it was a very old one.

We had two large freezers in our basement full of beef. Every cut of beef you can imagine, from the tongue to the rump. My father *loved* beef. He wanted to eat it every night, and we were required to eat what he ate. Beef, it's what was for dinner. Like Bubba Blue in *Forrest Gump*, we barbequed it, baked it, broiled it, sauteed it, and boiled it. My mother, being of German descent, rarely used spices. She was also frugal and wouldn't throw away old meat. So, we were often served meat that was years old and freezer burned. We ate more steak, pot roast, roast beef, flank steak, meat loaf, hamburgers, beef stew, and beef tongue than I care to remember. Needless to say, other than the occasional hamburger, I don't eat beef. Now you know why.

One beautiful summer day, not long after we had moved to Everett, my father decided that he wanted to have the entire family go for a bike ride in our neighborhood. Our home was situated atop Rucker Hill on Grand Avenue, and the street lived up to the name. Many of the homes on our street were elegant old mansions built by lumber barons surrounded by carefully manicured gardens. The homes on the west side of the street overlooked Port Gardner Bay.

This was 1972. I was four at the time and hadn't really taken to riding bikes yet. My siblings, then six and seven, were deemed by my father to be capable to ride their own bikes. I was placed in the child seat behind my father, which, unlike the child seats of today, did not offer a place to put my feet. Off we went on this arduous bike ride, with me being required to hold my legs out away from the spokes of the wheel for the entirety of the ride. We rode past Grand Avenue Park to the south, with breathtaking views of the sea, down a steep hill to Marine View Drive. Riding along the waterfront, the Great Northern Railroad tracks were on one side and the ocean, timber rafts, and Everett Yacht Club on the other. With trains going by, logging trucks, and other industrial vehicles competing for space on the road, this was a perilous endeavor.

As we made it back to the top of the hill and passed Legion Park, my legs began to cramp. I repeatedly *begged* my father to stop. "Daddy, P-L-L-L-E-E-A-S-E STOP! PLEASE! I need to rest! I can't hold my legs out any longer! My legs are K-I-L-L-L-L-I-N-G me! They are so tired! PLEASE, PLEASE, Daddy! PLEASE STOP!" My father answered in anger that we were almost home and to stop whining. And just as soon as he finished his reply, my legs collapsed, and the toes of my right foot caught the spokes of the wheel, ripping my ankle from its socket and twisting my foot around so that my foot was backwards. I screamed in agony as the spokes of the wheel bent and the bike came to a sudden halt. In the mangled wheel, I could see a bone protruding from my ankle and there was a visible chip in the bone. Blood was pouring from my leg. I wailed in horror and pain. My father extricated my foot from the spokes. He lifted me up and carried me into the closest house, a grand white mansion with four massive columns running along the front of the house. They were kind enough to let us in. As my blood spattered on their white floors, it stained their—and my—innocence. In that moment, I learned my father was not my protector; he hurt me. My father placed me in their kitchen sink, instructing my mother to let the water run over the wound as he rushed to get our station wagon to take me to the emergency room. I was hysterical. Like a broken and mangled doll, my foot dangled from my leg, but in the wrong direction.

I went home from the emergency room with a plaster cast on my leg, a scar on my ankle, a terror of riding bicycles, and a deep-seated anger toward my father. This was to become a pattern. My most basic physical needs were ignored because all that ever mattered was what my father wanted.

After the accident.

* * *

One winter morning, we all put on our Sunday best and set out for the First Presbyterian Church. First Presbyterian was the finest church in our city, and it was attended by our United States Senator, Henry "Scoop" Jackson, who lived down the street from us on Grand Avenue. I had a tummy ache that day, but that didn't matter to anyone. I put on the red velvet, floor-length dress that I had worn as a flower girl for my Aunt Helen's wedding, hoping that it might make me feel better.

As per usual, we got to church early so that we could sit up front. My father always wanted to be visible to the pastor. It was a busy

Sunday, so we crammed in like sardines in a can. We kids were expected to sit still and be quiet church mice. I tried, but my tummy was rumbling. "Mom," I whispered, "I need to go to the bathroom!" She shook her head "no" and held her finger up to her lips and shushed me. My tummy rumbled louder, and I was having little sharp pains. "Mommmmm!" I whispered more urgently, holding my tummy and squirming in my seat. She gave me a stern look and looked over at my father to see if he had noticed. "I need to go poop!" I declared. "Well, try letting out little toots and see if that helps," she instructed in a whisper. Ever the obedient child, I did as I was told.

As soon as the service let out, I ran to the ladies' restroom. I lifted my long dress and shit dripped everywhere. I gingerly took off my shit-soaked panties and dropped them into the female disposal bin where tampons usually go. I hopped on the toilet, but I was so slippery with shit, I shot off, smacked onto the floor and flew out of the stall. I crawled back into the stall and, gripping the underside of the toilet seat, held on as diarrhea thundered out of me. I was literally covered in diarrhea from the waist down. The inside of my dress had a thick coating of shit on it. I tried to scrape it off with toilet paper, but it was a lost cause. My pretty, white lace ankle socks were a lost cause too. I threw them away immediately. Would Mom be mad at me? I wasn't sure what to do. One lady came in and tried to help me to clean up. I did the best that I could, but my dress was soaked with diarrhea and the smell was overwhelming. No one came to look for me, so eventually I went out looking for my parents.

They were standing talking to a group of people in a circle. I approached timidly and grabbed my mom's skirt and gave it a tug.

"Mom, I need your help!" I whispered urgently. "Don't interrupt!" she replied, glancing at my father. Smelling me, she added, "Go wait in the car!" As I walked outside, my long dress dragged along the ground with the extra weight of the shit, leaving a trail like a slug. My brother and sister were already waiting in the car. They wouldn't let me in, I stank so badly. They pressed their freckled faces against the windows, holding their noses.

I sat on the cement curb, waiting for my parents to arrive, wrapping my arms around my body and shaking from fever and the cold. My tummy rumbled. I felt so alone. Eventually, my parents came out to the car, still engrossed in conversation. "Carrie, get in the car!" my father said angrily. "But they won't let me!" I said, pointing at my brother and sister who shook their heads "no" as they waved their arms in disgust. My father opened the back door and shoved me in next to my brother and sister. "What is that SMELL?" my father queried. My brother and sister pointed at me and held their noses. "It's stinky Carrie!" they said collectively. The windows were lowered as my brother and sister mimed gagging and throwing up. At home, I was stripped naked and put in the bath, left to bathe myself while my mother scurried around to get my father his lunch.

Between sharing a bathroom with my siblings, my fear of using public restrooms, and my father's expectations that I refrain from using the bathroom on command, I had unconsciously trained myself not to go to the bathroom. My first year of law school, I did not have a bowel movement for the entire month of law school exams. When I got severely constipated, I would subsist on Coca Cola—liquid energy. After law school exams were over, I took sixteen (sixteen!) Dulcolax to clean my body out. When I got married, my husband told me this was not normal. I was so disconnected from my body that I didn't even think I needed help. But at his urging, I saw a series of specialists and, at age twenty-five, had surgery to shorten my colon. It had simply stopped working.

It would be another decade before I realized how the trauma of my childhood had manifested in my body taking it literally. Understanding this lesson, I realized how critically important it is to deal with trauma and anger head-on. By stuffing things down and avoiding, I was harming myself physically.

* * *

As a child, I loved to cook. I had a *Betty Crocker Cookbook* filled with colorful illustrations that I loved to use to try out new recipes. One night, I asked my mom if I could make dinner for the family. Using my cookbook, I prepared a spaghetti dinner with garlic bread and salad. I set the table, put plates out, and filled the drink glasses, in eager anticipation of my father's arrival.

When cooking made me happy, before it didn't.

Every night my father would call my mother and let her know when he was on his way home from the hospital. The hospital was about five minutes from our house. No matter when that was, my mother was expected to have dinner on the table upon his arrival. This often meant cooking and reheating food. It was always a tense juggle to have dinner on the table precisely when he arrived. That night, I set dinner out "family style," so that we could pass the items and serve ourselves. My mother started to become tense as I set it out this way. "Maybe you should just dish some out for everyone?" she asked. "I'm not sure your father is going to like this." My mother normally plated everything in the kitchen so that when my father sat down, he had a full plate in front of him. Just then, we heard the garage door slam, announcing his arrival. We all scurried to sit down at the table. As he sat down, my mom explained that I had cooked dinner that evening. I was glowing with a sense of accomplishment as I handed him the Pyrex bowl of spaghetti. Grabbing it from me, all at once, he stood and hurled the bowl of spaghetti at the wall, shattering the Pyrex and sending spaghetti flying. "I TOLD YOU—I. WANT. DINNER. ON. THE. TABLE. WHEN I GET HOME!" he screamed. And with that, he pushed his chair back, knocking it over, and went back out through the garage, slamming the door behind him so hard that the wall shook. My mother gave me an angry look. "This is YOUR fault. Clean this mess up and go to your room!" I scurried around trying to quickly clean up the shattered Pyrex and spaghetti, apologizing profusely to my mother.

As you can imagine, I didn't cook much after that. I still don't. I joke that I'm great at making reservations. Years later, I sought out "healing hypnosis." My therapist guided me back to this memory. I was able to talk to my younger self. I told that little girl, "How sweet and thoughtful of you to make dinner for your father. That was such a loving gesture. You didn't do anything wrong. Your mother should have stood up for you and comforted you. The way that your father behaved was abusive and soul-crushing. He can't hurt you anymore." I gave my younger self a hug. This was so healing for me.

* * *

One cold and rainy night, I lay in my bed, straining to hear my sister's breathing over the hiss and ping of the radiator. I waited for the train below to pass and listened more carefully. She didn't sound so good. I climbed out of bed and walked across the room and stood next to her, putting my ear close to her mouth. She was definitely wheezing.

At age six, I had already experienced numerous emergency room trips to care for my sister's asthma. I understood the real life-and-death consequences of asthma and I had learned to recognize when my sister was in peril. Tiffany and I shared a room in part so that I could listen to her breathing. I had been given explicit instructions that night to listen to her breathing and if she started to wheeze, I was to go tell my father.

I tiptoed down the hall and down the stairs. As I neared my parents' bedroom, I saw that the door was ajar. I approached quietly. As I neared the doorway and was about to speak, I saw my mother kneeling before my father—both were naked. I let out a gasp. Both my parents looked up and then my father took off running after me. He was screaming, "What the hell are you doing out of bed? What are you doing out of bed?" I tore up the stairs as fast as I could run and jumped into my bed, covering myself with my bed covers. He wasn't far behind. He beat me through my bed covers. I was screaming and sobbing, "But I only came down to tell you that Tiffany was wheezing like you told me to…"

When he felt satisfied that he had gotten his message across, he quit and went back to bed. Tiffany peered out from under her covers. "What happened?" she asked. "I went down to tell him you were wheezing, and I saw him naked by accident," I whispered. "I'm sorry, sis," she said, shaking her head in disbelief while reaching for her inhaler. "I know." I cried myself to sleep.

I was the caretaker in the family. My brother was the brilliant one. My sister was the one who got special attention because of her asthma, her theatrics, her athleticism, and her rebelliousness. I learned that it was safest to operate in the shadows. I was the observer. I learned how to avoid trouble by watching my brother and sister. Most of all, I learned that getting attention equaled pain.

* * *

When I was about six years old, my father announced that we would be getting a puppy. I was overjoyed. I had been begging for a puppy for years. I had visions of a tiny pup that I could wrap in my arms. We drove our Volkswagen van out into the country to pick up our new dog from the breeder. I could barely contain my excitement as I waited for my father to retrieve our new puppy. The van door slid open and there sat, looking at me, a huge, scary-looking German Shepard. This was not a puppy! At six weeks old, this dog was taller than me when sitting! I felt that my father had tricked me. As per usual, he had gotten the dog that he wanted, not a dog that was suitable for young kids. We named the dog Suki and I watched her fearfully, unsure of what to make of her.

Turns out, Suki was very sweet. We spent a lot of time playing in the backyard and she was a constant companion. I would feed her under the table when my parents weren't looking. She would hide under the stairs with me when trouble was brewing. We developed a special bond.

One day, after a family outing, I discovered that Suki had chewed up one of my Barbies, tearing off a limb. I started to cry, exclaiming, "Suki ate my Barbie!" I held up my broken doll to show my father. He became enraged. I watched his face turn red, his eyes bulging. He grabbed Suki by the collar and dragged her outside. Retrieving a two-by-four from the wood pile, he began to beat Suki. My brother and sister and I watched through the French doors, screaming and pleading, "PLEASE, DAD! PLEASE, DAD! PLEASE STOP! STOP HITTING SUKI! I DON'T CARE ABOUT THE BARBIE! PLEASE JUST STOP!" He beat Suki again and again until the two-by-four broke in half, tossing it at the dog in disgust. He stormed into the house as I rushed out past him to find Suki. She had crawled away to hide in the cool dirt under some bushes. I went and held her, stroking her thick coat. "I am so sorry, Suki. I am so, so sorry," I whispered to her. I stayed with her until it turned dark and my mother insisted I come inside. Shortly thereafter, Suki disappeared. We were told that she had been taken to live on a farm. From that moment, my passion for dogs, particularly rescues, was born.

Me with my brother and our new puppy, Suki.

* * *

My father's violence controlled us. We lived in fear of his anger. He demanded total submission, and religion was his favorite weapon.

Not long after we moved to Everett, my parents became born-again Christians. Feeling out of control and out of water in a new community, my father saw Christianity as a means to control his world and others. We were the first victims. I recall a time the three of us children were forced down on our knees and told to pray as my father threatened us with a wood rod. He had a selection of paddles and rods that he created in his workshop and hung on the wall of the kitchen, ready for action. While we feared physical violence, his words did the most damage. My father was a master at manipulating scripture for his purposes. Among his favorite themes was that the wife must submit to the husband, and we were to honor him. His interpretation of these scriptures meant that he was the divine leader of our household, and we must surrender ourselves to him. He expected total submission. Total surrender of self meant subsuming our identities to him. This was his mission.

Years later, I picked up Susan Forward's *New York Times* bestseller *Toxic Parents* and recognized my family in the pages: "Unhealthy families discourage individual expression. Everyone must conform to the thoughts and actions of the toxic parent. They promote fusion, a blurring of personal boundaries, a welding together of family members. On an unconscious level, it is hard for family members to know where one ends and another begins. In their efforts to be close, they often suffocate one another's individuality."

I watched as my mother, who was once vibrant, creative, and fun, wilted under his tyranny. Anything that got in the way of her total submission to him was eliminated from her life. She gradually gave up neighborhood coffees, playing tennis, the piano, reading fiction, and most every other social outlet or hobby that brought her joy. She was expected to cater to him in every aspect of her life. If anything got in the way of that, it was eliminated. Indeed, my mother, Dorothy Louise Smith, who went by Dottie, would introduce herself as Mrs. Dr. John Smith. Dottie had disappeared.

My mother became depressed. She slogged through life. Isolated from family and friends, she immersed herself in the church, her only social outlet. The only books she read were the Bible and books about the Bible. She would not make decisions for herself, nor would she stand up for her children. Everything was about my father—what we ate, what we were allowed to do, where we went, what we believed, how we behaved—everything was decided by him.

My mother's identity was so subsumed by my father that all she had left of her identity was her physical body. The way that she would express her "self" was to talk about her physical ailments. This was her way of being in touch with her "self." My mother would talk about her menstrual cycle. She was having PMS. She was on her period. She was having *mittelschmerz*, a German word for one-sided, lower abdominal pain associated with ovulation that may occur about halfway through the menstrual cycle. She had migraines and would be in bed for days. As much as being hyperfocused on her physical body was my mother's last bastion to cling to her "self," it was also her way to get attention from my father, the Doctor.

He was so wrapped up in himself, he didn't see her. When I was four or five, I recall one evening when we all sat down at the dining room table to eat dinner and my mother got down on her hands and knees, complaining of abdominal pain. She was writhing in pain. We continued to eat our dinner. I pointed to my mother and said, "Dad, aren't you going to help her?" My father dismissed me. "I'm sure it's just gas. She'll be fine." He continued to eat his dinner. I took another look at my mother and volunteered, "I bet she's pregnant!" My mother remained on the floor and we cleared our plates and headed upstairs to bed. The next morning, we discovered that our mother was in the hospital. She had an ectopic pregnancy, and one of her fallopian tubes had burst. My father had to rush her to the hospital in the middle of the night for emergency surgery.

He didn't see me either. In elementary school, we traveled to San Francisco to visit an uncle. I had been complaining that my ears hurt, but I was told to stop complaining. On the flight, as we began our descent into San Francisco, I was overcome by pain. It felt like an ice pick was stabbing my eardrums again and again. I clutched my hands to my ears and let out a bloodcurdling scream. I couldn't stop screaming; the pain was like a continuous electrical current that got stronger by the minute. I was in agony. The flight attendant asked my father to get me to stop screaming—I was frightening the passengers. It sounded like I was being murdered. But I couldn't stop. My father pressed his hand over my mouth to muffle the sound, but it didn't help much. Once we landed, my father took his otoscope from his medical bag and looked in my ears. They were full of pus. I had a massive bilateral ear infection. I spent the remainder of the trip in the room at the Palace Hotel, popping antibiotics and painkillers and eating ice cream sundaes provided by my uncle. Later, in middle school, I was running a fever of 104.9 degrees for several days. My mother was giving me alcohol rubs and putting me in a cool bath to try to get my fever down. She begged my father to examine me. After a week with this high fever, my father looked down my throat and said, "Ahh, she has tonsilitis. I'll call in penicillin for her." A week of unnecessary suffering because he couldn't be bothered to look at me! I spent much of that week lying on a couch which was immediately next to my father's recliner, where he would sit after dinner each night and read his medical journals. I was literally inches away from him and yet he couldn't be bothered. What he was doing was more important.

My father didn't attend a single soccer game for my brother, tennis match for my sister, or dance recital for me. In fact, these activities didn't last long because they required our mother to pay attention to us, which took attention away from him. By second grade, there were no after-school activities for any of us. The loss made me immensely sad. My ballet teacher designated me her best student and gave me my own separate recital. She encouraged my parents to get me more lessons, but this was shot down by my father. Ballet lessons would interfere with his dinner.

My father loved to label us: "You're so ungrateful. You're so rebellious. You're so selfish." These labels never made sense to me. When we would go out to dinner, it would usually be to the Black Angus steakhouse. There was nothing on the menu that I liked to eat. Every time that we went there, I would eat a piece of bread and that would be it. I begged him to please let us go somewhere else, but he refused because it was his favorite restaurant. After the twentieth time of going out to dinner for a piece of bread, I said, "Dad, please, there is nothing there that I can eat! Going there and watching you all eat is torture for me!" To which he replied, "You are so selfish! You should be grateful that I'm taking you out to dinner!" I would ask him, "How am I being selfish?" His answers were nonsensical. I had an epiphany recently: I was being selfish when I was being myself! The moments when I disagreed with him, challenged him, expressed a desire to eat something different, or explored a hobby he didn't enjoy—I was literally being selfish! Realizing this, I called my sister, looking for clues—what was I doing when he called me selfish? To the present day, I am still trying to unearth the little girl who existed before he tried to mold me into his likeness.

Not only did my father label us, but he labeled others as well. When he would see a woman crossing the street whose outfit he did not approve of, he would say that she looked like a prostitute. Similarly, based just on appearance, he would decide if someone was a Christian or not. Every judgment he made served the purpose of putting him on a pedestal and putting others down. We began to see the world through his eyes. We became quick to judge and label.

We were isolated from mainstream society. My brother and sister and I attended a Christian school in Seattle (King's) until my brother graduated, my sister went to boarding school, and I transferred to a public high school. Other than school, our only other activities were skiing and church. When I arrived at public school, I was genuinely afraid of interacting with the "heathens" there. I was rigid, judgmental, and fearful. As judgmental as I was of others, I was ten times more judgmental of myself. I was filled with self-loathing. All that I could see were my imperfections. My father was always happy to point them out.

We attended numerous churches. At each church, my father would do things to get attention, insist on becoming a church elder, and eventually leave in frustration or be asked to leave. At Trinity Episcopal Church, my father oversaw the Sunday school program. From his perspective, this included disciplining children who acted up. I remember hearing loud whacks followed by the screams of children being paddled by my father in the Sunday school office. It wasn't long before we were gone. My father blamed it on the pastor, claiming that the pastor got caught drinking the communion wine. I had heard the kids screaming; I reached a different conclusion.

My father's religious views were constantly in flux. One year, Christmas was about celebrating Christ's birth. The next, it was a pagan and satanic holiday. One year we would have a Christmas tree and the next we would not. It was hard to keep up! He would interpret scripture to serve his agenda, which meant that his interpretations would often change.

My father loved to watch sports and war movies on television, so we had a TV. But he didn't like us watching television, so he was always trying to control our TV watching. He declared the TV "satanic" and severely limited our watching. One year, I came home from college and the TV didn't work. My father told me that it was broken. I suspected that he had disabled the TV on purpose. So, one afternoon when my parents left to run to Costco, I pulled the TV out from the wall and saw that several circuits had been disconnected. I reconnected the circuits and turned the TV on. When my parents returned from their errand, I was sitting there watching TV. My father walked into the room with his jaw hanging open. "Dad, look! The Holy Spirit fixed the TV!" I exclaimed. I knew I had him boxed in. He could not challenge me without admitting that he had lied and disabled the TV. With a look of shock on his face, he sat down and watched TV with me.

When I wanted to do something, I would ask my mother and she would say, "Let me check with your father." I would ask my father and he would say, "Let me pray about it." When a decision was made, my father would say, "I feel God telling me..." Consequently, I began to confuse my father's wishes with God's wishes. My father had a hotline to heaven after all. Whatever edict my father issued was final; he had already talked to God, so it was pointless to pray for a different outcome. In effect, he had cut me off from God.

My father was the sun. My mother, brother, sister, and I orbited around him. We all competed for his attention. I recall one period in my life when I was the favorite, from about five to seven years old. My father built me a wooden desk and a wooden go-kart. It was during this same period that we added on to our house; my father ignored my mother's input, instead letting me, a child, pick out the wallpaper for the master bedroom and bath. I was an innocent child being used in a cruel dynamic with my mother. Not getting the attention that she needed from my father, my mother began to spend more and more time with a woman from church named Judy. My mother flaunted the attention she was getting from Judy. When Judy sent my mother yellow roses for her birthday, my father became unhinged. He declared that the yellow roses were a romantic overture and that Judy had feelings for my mother. She was never allowed to speak to Judy again.

My father also pitted us against one another. One of us was always the black sheep. Whoever was the black sheep at that moment would have the rest of the family against him or her. Submit to his wishes, follow his divine teachings, or be cut off from the family. Susan Forward discussed this phenomenon in *Toxic Parents*. She wrote, "Many toxic parents compare one sibling unfavorably with another to make the target child feel that he's not doing enough to gain parental affection. This motivates the child to do whatever the parents want in order to regain their favor. This divide-and-conquer technique is often unleashed against children who become a little too independent, threatening the balance of the family system."

It wouldn't be until I married my second husband that I got serious therapy. I spent a year "on the couch" doing daily psychoanalysis. My very adept and caring therapist helped me to deprogram the damning messages from my childhood and guide me toward self-love. As I became less critical of myself, I became less judgmental. I gradually moved from anger to empathy.

For many years, I resented and complained about my father. Every time that I expressed my anger and resentment about my father, I gave him control again. Then, one day, I had an epiphany. Someone asked me what my greatest strength was, and I easily answered, "Intuition!" "Where do you think that gift comes from?" they asked. As I reflected on this question, I realized that my intuitive abilities were learned from walking on eggshells all the time. I had to develop a sixth sense to carefully navigate what might trigger my father. It was a survival skill that had been honed from years of living in terror. Intuition was my superpower. But it was the abuse of my father and the dynamic in our household that gave me that gift. I could not separate one from the other. *If I was to give thanks for the gift of intuition, I must also be grateful for the path that birthed it. I had arrived at a place of gratitude for my past. The resentment was gone, and I was free at last.*

While I received the gift of intuition to survive my childhood, my siblings each received different gifts. My brother received the gift of focus. He learned to escape into his mind. The world could be blowing up around him and he does not lose focus. My sister received the gift of fearlessness. While it scared the heck out of me, my sister would challenge my father. I will never forget the time that she walked up to him sitting in his armchair and told him to "fuck off." Then, she took off running. My father wasn't far behind. He went flying through the kitchen, ripping a rod from the wall. I hid as I heard my father beating the shit out of my sister. Yet, with each encounter she survived, her fearlessness grew. I attribute much of my sister's professional success to this quality. She really is fearless.

To be clear, it took me decades to recognize the gifts in my childhood. I first had to let myself acknowledge the pain, abuse, and neglect. I had to recognize it for what it was. Once I could put a label on it, I could view my experiences objectively. I needed to first experience rage before I could reach forgiveness. I needed to do the work to deprogram years of toxic messages. I needed to create a new internal dialogue—one of self-love instead of self-flagellation. And I could not forgive until I had established boundaries. I could only begin to forgive once I had protected myself from future harm. Then, I was able to recognize the good that was born out of the pain. I was also able to see that not everyone receives the same gift from the same experience. We all respond in different ways. This process moved me from being focused on myself and my pain to being focused on others and experiencing deep empathy. With this radical shift in myself, as more shit happened (because that is life and it just will), I began to view each new challenge with an eye for the opportunity or good within it. When Covid hit, I can honestly say that my immediate response wasn't one of fear. It was rather, "Bring it. I'm a survivor. I'm resilient. I can adapt. I'll get through this." Looking to history, I recognized that this is an exciting time: it is a huge opportunity for growth and innovation. Like entrepreneurs who seek first to identify a problem to solve it, I learned that it was important for me first to acknowledge that aspects of my life were shitty to see where the fertilizer was that I needed to bloom.

CHAPTER FOUR

COMPARISON KILLS

"Comparison is the thief of joy."

—THEODORE ROOSEVELT

From an early age, I was constantly compared to my sister,
Tiffany. I was told by my parents that Tiffany was better at ice skating, tennis, writing, and singing.

Around age eight, I asked my father, "Am I pretty?" He scrunched
up his face and spent a moment examining me more carefully. He
replied, "No. I don't want to give you false expectations or have
you disappointed in life." He reflected further, "But your sister?
Now, she is beautiful." These words were soul crushing. I felt my
self-esteem dissolve and evaporate. My father had told me "the
truth" that I was not pretty—in order to "protect" me. He also used
the comparison to my sister to set the standard for what beauty is.

I was told that I could not be myself and be beautiful. I must strive to be more like her and abandon my uniqueness.

My sister had beautiful curly hair and because mine was straight, I hated it. So, I started getting it permed. Imagine every photo you've seen of terrible perms in the 1980s. That was me. Trying to look more like my sister so that I could be more beautiful.

My sophomore year in college, our family went to St. Louis to spend Christmas with my paternal grandmother (Bahma), my father's sister, her husband, and our cousins. My cousin, Michael, was a member of a fraternity at Washington University and he took my sister and me to visit his frat house, along with his friend Alex. After a few beers, it became obvious that one of his frat brothers was totally enamored with my sister. As I watched her getting all of the attention, I found a couch to escape to. I pulled my legs into my chest and wrapped my arms around my legs, trying to make myself small, wishing I could disappear. Alex came over to comfort me. "I don't know how you do it. What is it like having a sister who is so beautiful? That must be so hard for you." I felt myself wither. I wanted to die.

After Christmas dinner, my grandmother took me aside. She was very observant and saw that I was depressed and really struggling. She handed me a small box. Inside the box was a charm. It was a mustard seed encased in glass. She said, "Carrie, you need to stop living in your sister's shadow. You need to follow your own path. Pursue your own interests." Taking the mustard seed out of the box, she placed it in my hand and rested her hand over mine. She looked me directly in the eyes and said, "Life is like a mustard seed. Have faith in yourself and you will grow into a strong tree and bear much fruit. But in order to grow, you need to plant yourself away from your sister's shadow." This was the greatest gift that my grandmother ever gave me. The tiny mustard seed charm, my most cherished gift. I had spent my entire life trying to be someone else. Her faith in me that I could chart my own course and grow into a vibrant being saved me and gave me the courage to begin to forge my own path.

My grandmother's words stayed with me, and over the years, I consciously chose to pursue interests and opportunities that were different from my sister's. I spent time discovering who I was and what I enjoyed instead of just doing the things that she did. I began to build self-esteem based on achievements that could not be compared to anything she was doing. (I went to law school. She went to business school.). Through these efforts, I reached the conclusion that one of us wasn't better than the other one. We are two unique individuals who both are beautiful, but for different reasons.

I began to observe who was receiving love and why. I observed that people were loved based on the likes, preferences, and values of others. One person wasn't necessarily more beautiful than another; rather, a person might prefer a blonde over a brunette or a curvy girl over a slim one. A person might receive love because of who they were, not because of how they appeared. "Beauty is in the eye of the beholder" may sound trite, but it is true. I began to understand that anyone who loved me would love me for *my* unique attributes. If they didn't appreciate me or find me beautiful, I simply wasn't *their* flavor of a person. Once I grasped this, rejection and comparison hurt less. I would tell myself: it's not that he doesn't like *me*; it's that I don't represent what he values as beautiful.

Twenty years after my grandmother gave me the mustard seed, I was with a girlfriend who was a former Miss Austin. We were having coffee with a local CEO. When she left the table to use the restroom, he said to me, "What is it like hanging out with her? She's so beautiful. It must be hard for you, her getting all of the attention all of the time." His words ripped the scab off an old wound. Really? Again? WTF?! I looked him in the eyes and replied, "Wow, what's it like putting your foot in your mouth all of the time? Saying thoughtless things must get you into a lot of trouble. And, by the way, I hold my own just fine. There are plenty of people who find me beautiful." I watched him realize his idiocy. As he turned beet red and began to sputter apologies, I excused myself and took my coffee outside. Sitting outside on a bench, I took some deep breaths. His words hurt, but after years of hard work, I knew my value. My tree was growing stronger.

CHAPTER FIVE

FAMILY REJECTION

"Rejection is the sand in the oyster, the irritation
that ultimately produces the pearl."

—BURKE WILKINSON

In our family, tennis was incredibly important. My maternal grandmother, Mimi, had grown up playing tennis. So, my mother and her siblings played, and their spouses played, and my cousins played. My parents maintained their membership at the prestigious Merion Cricket Club in Haverford, Pennsylvania, for years after moving to the West Coast. As soon as we moved to Everett, Washington, my mother joined the Everett Racquet Club and enrolled us in tennis lessons.

I recall hours upon hours of tennis lessons. Initially, I did okay, but my performance seemed to worsen after about a year of lessons. I was struggling to hit the ball. My tennis instructor was very impatient with me, yelling at me to "keep my eye on the ball." Frustrated with me, he often left me to practice my serve over and over again by myself. Honestly, if I had one dollar for every time I was told to "keep my eye on the ball," I would be a rich woman.

No doubt, I sucked. Swing and miss. Swing and miss. Swing and miss. It was embarrassing and also frustrating, because trust me, I was keeping my eye on the ball. My mother was embarrassed; my siblings teased me. Eventually, my mother told me that it just didn't make sense to pay for lessons for me anymore. I was ashamed, but relieved.

The other sport of primary importance in our family was figure skating; one of my uncles even went to the Olympics for figure skating, and an aunt competed at nationals. Everyone from my grandma to my cousins skated, so I was enrolled in skating lessons at five years old along with my sister. At eighteen months my senior, she was naturally better coordinated than I was. At five years old, I was like a puppy sliding all over, discovering what I was capable of. Once again, it was decided that they would continue with lessons for Tiffany, but not for me.

As the years passed, my maternal cousins established themselves as national squash champions, expert tennis players, Olympic-hopeful-level skaters, and collegiate soccer players. I became a straight-A student who loved to read and avoided anything athletic. This would come back to haunt me.

In Grandmother's world, you were either adored and doted on or shamed and discarded. My grandmother had attended Miss Porter's School in Farmington, Connecticut. My mother had attended Miss Porter's as well, so they decided that my sister should go, too. Not me. My mom and Mimi fawned over Tiffany, excited to share their experience with her. When Tiffany graduated, my grandmother hosted a huge reception for our entire extended family at the Merion Cricket Club. The plan was for the entire extended family—all eighteen of us—to play in a tennis round-robin, followed by a reception and dinner.

The three MPS girls: my sister, mother, and grandmother at Miss Porter's School.

My sister receiving a special graduation gift from my grandmother on her graduation day from Miss Porter's School.

Tennis Round Robin at Merion Cricket Club.

We all donned our tennis whites and headed out onto the grass courts. I headed to the farthest court to try to avoid notice. My grandmother oversaw the play and, after a few minutes, pointed at me and began to screech, "YOU. YOU. YOU CAN'T PLAY TENNIS! GET. OFF. THE COURT! GET OFF THE COURT, *NOW!*" Time slowed down. I looked around. My entire family had stopped playing tennis and was staring at me. With disdain. With shame. With horror. With pity. I turned beet red and began to shake as a knot grew exponentially in my stomach. "HURRY UP. OFF THE COURT, NOW!! YOU KNOW YOU CAN'T PLAY TENNIS," she continued. My parents looked at me with shame, embarrassed that I was their child. No one, not one family member, interceded on my behalf. I scurried off the court, red-faced and in tears, hoping to avoid more wrath from my grandmother.

My grandmother had made it clear: I was worthless and did not belong in our family. Her rejection so harsh and complete, it left me breathless and cascaded me into darkness. The entire family assembled to celebrate my sister and at the same time, I was discarded. It was clear that to be kind or compassionate to me was to cross the matriarch of the family. No one dared to do that, not even my parents.

Years later, in law school, I began to develop double vision. During my summer clerkship in Atlanta, I noticed that when I would drive home at night, I would see one speedometer on top of another. It was difficult for me to read, as the words appeared to be stacked on top of each other. I went to see a specialist who diagnosed me with a sixth cranial nerve palsy. He said that the additional eye strain from law school had likely exacerbated it. He also confirmed that I most likely had lived with this condition for years. Since I did not have any of the primary conditions that were likely to cause this, the doctor asked me if I had ever suffered trauma to my eye. As I reflected back, I could only remember one incident where I had received a black eye.

When I was about five years old, my sister and I were standing on our back deck when Christopher, a boy who lived next door to us, wandered into the yard. He wanted to play with us. My sister enjoyed taunting him, so she told him that she would give him what was in her right hand if he pulled down his pants and showed us his pee-pee. My sister displayed two Oreo cookies in her right hand. He pulled down his pants and showed us his pee-pee, demanding the cookies from my sister. While he was pulling down his pants, my sister had put her hands behind her back and switched the cookies to her left hand. She then displayed her empty right hand to him. "Look, they disappeared!" she exclaimed. Seeing that he had been tricked, Christopher picked up a rock and threw it at my sister. Unfortunately, he missed her completely and hit me in the eye instead.

While I giggled as I thought about this story, the world suddenly made sense. The doctor explained to me that with this condition, one eye might see an image at four feet and the other at six feet—my brain would then fuse the images together to make one image. When I looked at a tennis ball, and I mean really *had my eye on the ball*, one eye would see it at one height and the other at another. When a ball is coming at me quickly, it is especially difficult for my brain to merge the images and for me to swing and hit it.

The timing of the injury also explained why I suddenly got worse at tennis. I wasn't defective. I had been injured. For some reason, this distinction allowed me to be compassionate toward myself. I mean, who berates an injured person for not being able to play a sport? That's just cruel.

With my diagnosis in hand, I told my parents that I wanted to spend that Christmas with Mimi at her winter house in Florida. I was convinced that if Mimi understood *why* I sucked so hard at tennis, she would be able to love me.

I arrived in Florida excited to see that my Aunt Betty, Uncle Charlie, and cousins Garrett and Reade were there too. I idolized them. Betty was a trailblazer; she was one of the first women to make the executive ranks on Wall Street. Similarly, my Uncle Charlie held a top job at a Wall Street bank. He was chairman of the board of trustees of the venerable Hill School where he, my cousins, uncles, and grandfather had attended. Garrett and Reade were now at Yale, following in their father's and grandfather's footsteps. National squash champions in their respective years and expert tennis players, Garrett and Reade were the apple of my grandmother's eye: they could do no wrong. Because of this, they loved to engage in hijinks. Over the years we had bonded over sneaking cocktails at the country club and joking around.

On this trip, Mimi had arranged for everyone to go to her country club to play golf and have lunch. When we arrived at the club, Mimi decided who would play with whom. Turning to me, she said, "You'll just have to wait at the club." Anger welled up inside me. Here we go again. Garrett and Reade were sitting in their golf cart ready to go and they motioned to me to come along. I hopped in the cart with them and as we sped off, I felt my heart leap with a mixture of freedom, joy, and fear. My grandmother began to scream, "GET OFF THE COURSE! GET OFF THE COURSE! YOU DON'T KNOW HOW TO PLAY GOLF!" I began to shake with fear and a huge knot started to build in my stomach. I was defying my grandmother. Her wrath was sure. Yet, as we zipped away, I also felt my heart soar, experiencing the freedom of being me.

When we returned to the club, my grandmother continued to berate me. She made it clear that I was not one of them. In her eyes, I didn't cut it. She was ashamed of me. Back at her house, I grabbed a book and retreated to a nook to read. She came and found me. "Why are you reading? What a waste of time. You should be doing something active!" she said with disdain. I loved to read. She didn't value having a granddaughter who was smart and attended a top law school. Nor did she value having a granddaughter who was kind, quick-witted, and creative. She didn't value me or my uniqueness. I simply didn't fit in my family.

A few years later, my grandmother invited all of her children and grandchildren on a cruise—except for my siblings and me. My mother told me that she and my father were going on the cruise, though. I was stunned. I felt betrayed. How could my parents sell us out so easily? Why didn't they stand up for us and insist that they wouldn't go unless their children were invited too? I was shocked that Tiffany wasn't invited. She was one of Mimi's favorites. Did she dislike me so much that she decided if she wasn't going to invite me that she wouldn't invite all three of us children? These questions remain unanswered, but I can tell you that my parents and all of my aunts, uncles, and cousins went on that cruise. I felt abandoned, my expulsion from the family complete.

In hindsight, being separated from the pack gave me freedom to be who I am. I wasn't like them, so I didn't have to try to be like them. My self-esteem isn't based on being a part of this family. It's based on being me. My grandmother's rejection released me from participating. It allowed me to pursue my own dreams and to stop living to meet the expectations of my family.

CHAPTER SIX

MONEY, MEN & MARRIAGE

*"A girl must marry for love and keep on
marrying until she finds it."*

—ZSA ZSA GABOR

Given my family history, there was an enormous emphasis placed on money, wealth, and social status. After the death of my maternal grandfather, my grandmother, Mimi, married Norman Davidson, who had extensive holdings in oil, gas, and real estate throughout the United States. They lived in Kennett Square, Pennsylvania, on a massive farm and ranch called Dalkeith. Dalkeith featured a half-mile tree-lined driveway that ended at the main house—a three-story colonial home built in the 1700s. There were numerous barns, stables, a caretaker's cottage, and other outbuildings, as well as a pond stocked with fish, hundreds of black angus cattle, and a slew of show horses and Welsh ponies. Grandpa Norm would sometimes hitch the horses to a carriage and drive us around the ranch to see its beauty. As picturesque as this property was, the main house reflected Norm's Quaker beliefs—it was simple and functional and lacked the luxurious finishes, grandeur, and glamour of the homes where Mimi had spent her early years. After Norm's death, Dalkeith Farm became a much sought-after subdivision. While he lived, there were often family events at Dalkeith. As much as I was enchanted by Dalkeith, I feared going there because Grandpa Norm was as mean as he was rich. He would yell at my grandmother for some perceived indiscretion and then she would yell at us (often in German). To avoid Norm's wrath, my grandmother started hosting family gatherings away from Dalkeith in places like The Cloister in Sea Island, Georgia, and Tanque Verde Ranch in Tucson, Arizona. My grandmother would take us to the most exclusive clubs and to dine at the finest restaurants. Our manners had to be perfect or we were sure to experience her wrath. This was the backdrop of my life. The expectation was that we were to live in this fashion; putting up with the abuse and tyranny of others to achieve this lifestyle was understood to be part of that path.

Following in my grandmother's footsteps, my mother married my father because she thought that marrying a doctor would provide social status and economic security. Unfortunately, my father loved to spend money as fast as he made it, which meant constant fights about our finances. One of my father's favorite phrases was, "We can't afford it!" Yet, there was always money for things that conveyed status—a home on the waterfront, private schools, luxury vacations—but I was forced to use the same set of towels for thirteen years and my comforter and sheets from childhood were never replaced. My parents would donate piles of money to establish themselves as leaders in the church, but, for years, I went without a proper winter coat. I couldn't reconcile how this made sense. Why was everyone else more important than me, their own daughter? Didn't they love me? My mother did not want to devote the time or money to properly clothe my sister or me. Her solution was to put my sister and me on a clothing allowance of fifty dollars a month when we reached eighth grade. This amount was expected to cover everything—coats for rain, ski jackets, winter coats, sweaters, clothing for school, dresses for church, eating out and other events, shoes, swimwear—everything. We were supposed to dress according to their standards on $600 a year. This amount did not come close to covering all that we needed, especially because discount retailers were not yet available in our area, and the only places my mother took me to shop were the department stores Nordstrom and the Bon Marché. I started working in my father's office at age fourteen to supplement this allowance. At sixteen, I took jobs at Nordstrom and the Squire Shop selling men's clothing and at a local seafood restaurant, Pelican Pete's, busing tables. My parents bought me a used car so that I could drive to school and my various jobs.

My father would tell us that we were better than others because of our wealth and social status. "We" did or didn't do certain things because of who "we" were. Yet, I wasn't part of the "we." My brother and sister were. My father paid for everything for my brother, including the tuition and expenses for him to receive bachelor's and master's degrees from Stanford University. He also paid for my sister to attend high school at Miss Porter's boarding school in Connecticut and college at the University of Southern California.

My parents asked me to transfer to public high school and to attend a state university so that they could afford to pay for my brother and sister. I had excellent grades and test scores but was not allowed to even apply to Yale or any other school. My parents told me that I would not qualify for tuition assistance because of their income. So, I applied to Washington State University (at least it was on the other side of the state from my parents) and was admitted with distinction to the Honors Program.

One summer in college, I worked three jobs. I worked full-time at the front desk of the local Holiday Inn. Those shifts ran from 7 a.m. to 3 p.m. Then, I would leave the Holiday Inn and go to the Mukilteo Chop and Oyster House to bus tables from 4:30 p.m. to 10:30 p.m. four days a week. I also did medical billing coding at my father's office. At the end of a long summer of hard work, I had enough money to buy a plane ticket to Tulsa, Oklahoma, to visit my best friend from high school, who was establishing residency to attend Oklahoma State University. It was a well-deserved vacation. I was exhausted from my hard work.

As I was leaving to go to the airport, my father stopped me. He was red-faced and angry. "I think that if you can afford to fly to Oklahoma, you can pay for your car insurance," he said. The front door was open, and my mom was waiting for me to bring my bags out. I stared at him in disbelief. Was he fucking kidding? I had already sacrificed so much so that he could pay for everything for my brother and sister. I had worked three jobs all summer and now he wanted to take the money that I had earned from me? He had never even mentioned anything about me paying for car insurance. Not ever. Why now, as I am walking out the front door? He stood with his hands on his hips, glaring at me. He was not going to let me out the front door. What the holy fuck?! The only gift of any value that my father had given to me was a gold cross with a diamond in the center. I moved past him and ran up the stairs to my room. I grabbed the gold cross and ran back down the stairs. I shoved it in my father's face and said, "This should cover my car insurance!" I tossed the necklace at him in disgust. "Come on, Mom, or I'll miss my flight." Unsure of what to do, my mother followed me out to the car and drove me to the airport. My father never brought up the car insurance again.

After I transferred to The University of Texas at Austin, I worked at the dean of students' office and my parents paid my rent and gave me $150 a month for my electric, phone, groceries, and whatever other essentials I needed. It wasn't enough. By the end of the month, I was eating butter and crackers.

When it came time to apply to law school, my parents said it was my turn and to go wherever I would like. When I was accepted to Tulane University School of Law, my parents encouraged me to go even though the tuition was steep. Shortly after I arrived at Tulane, my parents called to tell me that they had changed their minds. "We've decided that we are done paying for things for you kids. So, we've decided that we won't be paying for your law school after all," my father proclaimed. Say what? Was I hearing him right? I pleaded with him, "But what about your promise to me? I went to public school and state university to help out. I would have gone to a state school if I'd known you were going to do this! You are still claiming me on your income tax! I won't qualify for any need-based grants or loans!" My pleas fell on deaf ears. The decision had been made. My only option was to get the more expensive credit-based loans with interest rates of 8–12 percent annually. They had thoroughly fucked me. I didn't just feel abandoned. I felt screwed. I scrambled to line up what loans I could and went to work for Professor Carbonneau as a research assistant.

I got used to being hungry. I would look at the money that I had and map out what I could afford to eat. One day, I was at the local supermarket purchasing a canister of powdered SlimFast and a gallon of milk. I determined that SlimFast had added vitamins and nutrients and by combining the two, I would have my meals for the week. In front of me in line was a woman using food stamps. She had packed the conveyer belt with pork chops, potatoes, sausage, vegetables, bread, cakes, and more. I called my father in tears. "Dad, the woman in line using food stamps has more food to eat than I do!" I cried. "I'm working and going to school and can only afford a canister of SlimFast and milk!" Without missing a beat, my father replied, "You know, I hadn't thought of that. You could always apply for food stamps!" Say what? My father never missed an opportunity to condemn people on welfare. He loved to rail on people who needed public assistance. Suddenly, he thinks it's a great idea for me to go on food stamps just to alleviate his guilt for leaving me high and dry? Was he kidding? Sadly, he was not. "Dad, I'm not going to apply for food stamps. That is ridiculous!" I sobbed. "Well, that is up to you!" he replied.

In 1992, during my second summer of law school, I clerked in Atlanta, making $1,000 a week. However, right before I left for my clerkship, I was having terrible problems with my ears and had tubes inserted in them. I had been plagued with ear problems my entire life. As a young child, I would pick at my ears until they were bloody and scabbed, trying to clear them. I was taken to a specialist only once, who told me to stop picking at my ears! Living in New Orleans, the mold got the better of me and I constantly had fluid in my ears. The tubes brought me some relief, but at a heavy cost. I only had student health insurance and it didn't cover much. Between my rent in Atlanta and New Orleans, and my medical bills, there wasn't much left over. Once again, I determined exactly how much money I had and plotted out my meals. I purchased a six-pack of blueberry muffins, thinking that would equal six breakfasts, but after the third day the muffins were covered in mold. I stood in the kitchen looking at the muffins and feeling like they had betrayed me. Green fuzzy mold danced across their tops. I pulled a muffin out to see if I could eat a portion of it, but the green fuzz had spared no part. I held the muffin and sobbed, tossing them all in the garbage. My stomach rumbled from hunger. I called my mother and told her how I was struggling. She said that she would send me a care package. A few days later, I opened the manilla envelope that she had sent to me. Inside was a bottle of Centrum and a box of granola bars along with a note that said she was praying for me. Not exactly the help I had hoped for.

My father called me and told me to stop asking them for help. He told me that I should ask the church for help. He encouraged me to write to my Uncle Charlie and ask him for help. "Charlie and Betty have tons of money. They work on Wall Street. He manages your grandmother's money. Write him a letter and ask him for help!" he commanded. I was desperate. There was something wrong with the tubes in my ears. I couldn't clear my ears anymore. I was in constant pain. I was hungry. I was mentally, spiritually, and emotionally defeated. Desperate people do desperate things. I am embarrassed to admit it—but I asked the church for money and they gave me $2,000. I wrote to my Uncle Charlie. His reply pierced my soul. "While it is too bad that your father did not save enough for his own daughter's education, it is not our responsibility to make up for his deficiencies. We are sorry, but we cannot help." I was humiliated. My father had set me up.

As the summer of 1992 ended, I had a second surgery on my ears. They had originally placed metal tubes in my ears. My ears had a massive reaction and had filled with scar tissue. The doctor removed the scar tissue and replaced the tubes with plastic ones. Finally, I had some real relief, but I also had more medical bills. My mother helped me to secure some supplemental medical insurance through Blue Cross Blue Shield in case something else happened. I returned to working as a research assistant, determined to finish law school.

In September of that year, my sorority big sister from WSU came to visit me. She had never been to New Orleans before and wanted to visit the French Quarter. Tulane University is located in the Uptown area of New Orleans. As students, we tended to socialize in the Uptown area and rarely ventured out in the French Quarter where all the tourists flocked. Colleen and I landed at a club called Rhythms. As we waited in line to enter the gated courtyard where the jazz band was playing, we encountered a guy sitting on a stool checking IDs. He gave me the once-over, took us to our table, and insisted on buying our drinks. As we went to leave, he asked for my phone number. Reluctantly, I gave it to him. Colleen: "Wow, he was totally into you! Would you go out with him?" I said, "No way. I don't want to date some guy who works on Bourbon Street!" Colleen flew back to New York City and I focused on law school. Well, the guy on Bourbon Street was very persistent and I eventually agreed to go on a date.

Beaux took me to some of the finest restaurants in New Orleans. As hungry and broke as I was, he got to my heart through my stomach. A few months later, we were eating dinner at Emeril's restaurant and he surprised me by getting down on one knee and proposing. I stared at him in disbelief. Was this really happening? People in the restaurant were staring. I felt the pressure from their gaze to say "yes." In shock, I excused myself and ran to the restroom where there was a pay phone. I called my best friend from high school and asked her what I should do. "I'm not going to say either way," she replied, "because if I tell you what to do and it doesn't work out, you will blame me." I so desperately wanted her to say, "Don't do it! What are you, crazy? You can do better than him!" Instead, I was left staring at the phone. I knew I didn't love him, but I was so alone. I felt like I had been abandoned by my family. No one gave a shit about me, but Beaux did. Plus, I didn't want to embarrass him. I had left him waiting at the table. There was no way this was going to happen, anyway. My father would never approve of Beaux. I returned to the table and said, "Yes." Beaux turned to the diners in the restaurant. "She said yes!" The diners around us began to clap and cheer.

Beaux was over-the-moon excited. I immediately felt regret. We arranged to travel to Everett so that he could meet my parents. I was counting on my father to torpedo the engagement. I was convinced that there was no way my snobby, elitist, fundamentalist Christian father would approve of my marriage to a bar manager from Bourbon Street. Did I mention that he smoked, and my father is a lung doctor?

Beaux went to lunch alone with my father and came back victorious. "Damn, you had me so nervous! He put his arm around me and said, son, she is your responsibility now! Fuck, he practically gave me your birth certificate!" While Beaux was overjoyed, I felt my world close in on me. My father wanted nothing to do with me. I was being discarded.

As we approached Christmas of 1992, my father announced that he had sold the office building that he co-owned with several other doctors. He was taking my mother to Maui to celebrate and wanted me and my sister to come. I remember receiving my airline ticket and looking at the cost. I would have rather that he sent me some much-needed cash. My sister and I traveled to meet my parents in Maui. They rented a one-bedroom timeshare with a fold-out couch for my sister and me to sleep on. My father's idea of vacation was sitting on the beach and reading. Tiffany and I would walk to the Westin next door and lay out on the beach in front of the resort. We were bored out of our minds. Neither one of us had any money and all my father wanted to do was eat in the condo and read. We were in Maui, but not allowed to experience it. It was pure torture. After days of this, my father decided that we should go snorkeling. On this day, my sister and I observed the strangest behavior we'd ever seen. My mother pranced about as if she had won a big contest. She was flaunting the attention that she was getting from my father. We were trapped and forced to watch my mother's victory lap. My sister and I discussed this odd behavior. "WTF, Mom is acting so strangely! Why is she flaunting the attention she is getting from Dad?" I asked. Tiffany agreed. "Why is she acting like she is on her honeymoon? It's just bizarre. It makes me feel so uncomfortable!" They wouldn't give us any money to go do our own thing, so we were a captive audience—and they seemed to enjoy that. As I reflected on my mother's behavior,

I realized that my father's decision not to pay for my law school was a victory for her. She would be the only subject of his love and his finances.

As I approached the end of my third year of law school, I developed a terrible and bizarre condition: fluid began to drip, then pour, out of one of my ears—by the cup full. When I woke up one morning with my pillowcase drenched in fluid, we decided I needed to go to the emergency room. I was in the middle of finals, but I was having excruciating headaches and the amount of fluid coming out made it impossible to sit through an exam. At the ER, the doctor could not decide if I had an ear infection or if I had a cerebral spinal fluid leak. The amount and color of the fluid were perplexing him. To rule out a cerebral spinal fluid leak, contrast dye was injected into my spinal cord and I was strapped onto a table and tilted upside down while an X-ray was taken. When the doctor injected the contrast dye, he hit my spinal cord. Talk about next-level pain—I was in total agony. Pain shot through my legs as I begged for relief. I was admitted to the hospital and injected with Demerol every four hours.

The doctors were still confused about what was going on, so I asked Beaux to call my father and let him know that I was in the hospital. I was hoping that he would speak to my doctors. Beaux spoke to my father and then handed me the phone. "He wants to talk to you." I pressed the phone to my good ear. "Your mother and I have been talking and we think it is really important that you know that we are not paying for this." And then he was gone. I sat staring at the phone as tears burned my eyes. His abandonment of me was complete. No visit, no concern, no words of comfort, no flowers, no card, no "get well soon." Just, "We're not paying for this."

There are moments in time that are like a light switch, a before and after. This was one of those moments for me. The little girl, the daughter who desperately wanted her father's love, she died that day. But resolve and fight were born. I would show him that I could be successful without his love or support.

I was in the hospital for five days. When I left the hospital, they were still unsure of what had caused all of the fluid, but by blasting my body with antibiotics and steroids, my ear had dried up. I was still in great pain. Beaux said that with my hunched-over slow walk I looked like I was "one generation out of the jungle." He drove me from the hospital directly to the justice of the peace. I didn't even know where he was taking me. I still had Demerol pulsing through my veins. I was so drugged that I barely recall being there, much less getting married. After the ceremony, we went back to campus. I took my last final and graduated from law school as if nothing changed. We told no one what we had done. My parents had agreed to pay for my wedding, and we were going to make them pay. Eventually, I confided in my sister, who was my maid of honor, to which she replied, "So wait, then I'm just a prop?"

My mother came for my law school graduation. She wanted to dine at some of the famous restaurants in New Orleans, go shopping for herself, and tour the Garden District. I was in no shape for any of those things. She behaved like a tourist on holiday. Her visit was all about her, not about caring for me or celebrating my graduation. I finally asked her, "Mom, what are you guys going to get me for graduation?" I was hoping for a briefcase, the perfect gift for a young lawyer. She chuckled. "Me! I'm your graduation gift! The money we are spending on my trip—that's your graduation gift!" I choked back tears as I thought, *I wish you hadn't come.*

Beaux and I moved to Austin and began to plan our August wedding in Seattle, while pretending to live separately. I studied for the bar exam and consulted with my mother on wedding items. Since I was a young child, my parents had told me that I would be inheriting my paternal grandmother's diamond necklace. The necklace was kept in a vault at the bank. It was stunning, with diamonds all the way around. I brought up the necklace to my mother. "Mom, I would really love to wear Bahma's necklace at my wedding. Can we get it out of the vault?" My mom replied haughtily, "Oh, we gave that necklace to the church. We thought it might be a stumbling block for you." "What? You gave my inheritance to the church? Without even discussing it with me? So, what, the pastor's wife is now sporting a new diamond necklace?" I shook my head with incredulity. My family was so fucked up.

My father told me that I was not allowed to put an engagement or wedding announcement in the local paper. He explained that while I was off at law school, he had testified before the Washington State Legislature offering his opinion as a physician that homosexuality was not natural; it was an abhorrent behavior that could be altered through conversion therapy. He had been receiving death threats and was concerned that if the date and location of my wedding were published, protestors might show up and mar the occasion. I resented the fact that my father's outrageous behavior was once again negatively impacting my life.

We were married (again) on an August evening at sunset on a yacht on Puget Sound. My father would not allow the bars on the two upper decks to serve drinks to my guests. We were all under his control. We were trapped on a boat with no liquor. My guests understood my distress and invaded the party on the deck below us to purchase drinks from their bar. My sweet friend Allison made it her mission to make sure that I had a constant flow of drinks. I learned over the years that the more that my father tried to control me, the more creative I would become to subvert his control. Thankfully, I had friends who understood the dynamic. Beaux and I spent our honeymoon night in Seattle. We traveled back to Austin where Beaux tended bar and worked some other inauspicious jobs while I began working as an associate at a law firm.

It was time to start paying off my student loans, hospital bills, and related credit card debt—all told, I owed $150,000. Beaux would joke about me being "his golden ticket," but I barely made enough to cover our bills. Beaux liked to party, drink, and smoke cigarettes and pot. We constantly fought about his smoking. Beaux promised to give up both cigarettes and pot when we got married, but I would come home to a dead-bolted front door. Once he unlocked the door, I would walk into a room that reeked of cigarettes and marijuana. It was infuriating that he was so inconsiderate. I was focused on starting my new career in law. I didn't want to have to worry about getting pulled over with marijuana in the car and have my hard-earned law license in jeopardy. We constantly fought and it wasn't long before Beaux started punching in walls and doors, screaming and throwing things at me.

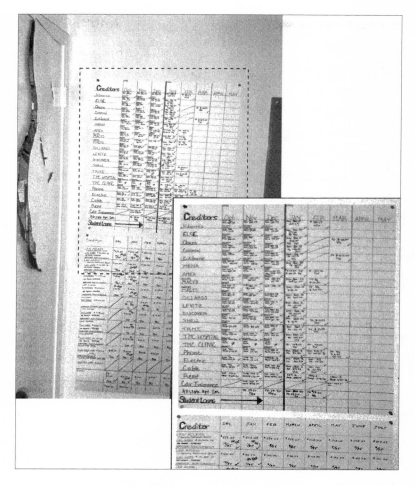

We didn't have Quicken then, so I put all of our bills and my student loans on a chart to keep track. All of the doors in the apartment looked like the one on the left: broken and punched in.

He would push me into the wall or onto the bed regularly. He once threw the remote at me and it slammed into the wall with such force that it entered the wall like a missile where it remained stuck in the wall for days. As his violence increased, I knew I needed to divorce him. However, I was still under the spell of my parents and believed that when you marry, it's for life. I was worried about their wrath and shame. I was angry at my father for giving his blessing to a man who I so clearly should not have married. I started having conversations with God and came to believe that in no way was this what God had intended for me. I summoned up the courage to file for divorce.

Five months after my divorce from Beaux was final, I met my second husband, Jason. At the time, Jason represented everything to me that Beaux was not. He was smart, educated, and came from a good family. He had impeccable manners and was a man of character.

After briefly sharing a home with a couple of girlfriends, I moved to a small apartment with a bed, a TV, and a table. I reduced my expenses as much as possible and focused on paying off my debts. I rewarded myself at the halfway point with a couch. When they were all paid off, I got a car with power steering and power windows. My student loans had been like a foot on my throat, strangling me. Being free from this heavy debt shifted my perspective from barely surviving to knowing my power. I could make it on my own.

After two years of dating, I was ready to get married, but Jason was not. I was heartbroken. I broke up with him, saying, "Look, you've had long enough to sample the goods, you know what you are going to get!" A month later, he came back to me and said, "I want to marry you. But I want to ask you in my own way and at my own time." It was May 1998; I told him that he had until Labor Day, and if he didn't propose by then, we were done. He invited me to go on a Crystal cruise to Alaska with his mother, sister, and stepfather in

July. About halfway through the cruise, we disembarked in Juneau, Alaska. After drinks at the Red Dog Saloon, Jason and I took a helicopter to Mendenhall Glacier. As we walked around the glacier, our guide warned us about a nearby crevasse. I noticed out of the corner of my eye that Jason was suddenly on the ground. I reached for him, panicked that he was falling into the crevasse. As I turned to face him, I realized that he was actually down on one knee and holding out a ring. My terror turned into surprise and then joy. This was the moment. He was asking me to marry him! I was overjoyed! I immediately said yes, but in that split second my quick wit voiced a thought: *If this goes poorly, suddenly I'm the ice queen!*

I was thrilled to be engaged to Jason and as I got to know his mother, Elizabeth, I fell hard for her too. I knew that Elizabeth had been an alcoholic, but in her ten years sober, she was trying to make up for it. We had a lot in common. We were both members of the Junior League, and she was the president of her chapter. We read the same books, liked the same fashion, and enjoyed the same things. Her daughter, Heather, was bohemian and creative—she acted on a soap opera, worked as a stunt woman, and played poker professionally. Beautiful, brilliant, and creative, Heather was very different from her mother and because of this, also very misunderstood. Elizabeth and I bonded because she was the mother that I never had, and I was a daughter she understood. She was so thoughtful and generous with me. She took Jason, Heather, and me on some amazing five-star luxury vacations. I wrote her heartfelt thank-you notes. I had so much gratitude for her and our relationship. I genuinely cherished it.

Jason and I were married on Grand Cayman Island on June 5, 1999, with about forty of our close friends in attendance. Jason and I paid for our own wedding and Elizabeth hosted a beautiful rehearsal dinner. Of course, my father called to tell me that he wasn't paying for any of this. We assured him that we didn't want his money. He and my mother attended the wedding (which, of course, had an open bar!). After a honeymoon in Aruba, Jason and I embarked on our new life.

The first few years of our marriage were pure bliss. We bought a house in the exclusive gated neighborhood of Rob Roy and began to renovate it. We enjoyed some amazing trips with his mother. But in June of 2002, Jason's father died from bladder and colon cancer. Up to this point, Jason had been ambivalent about having children. His parents divorced when he was young, but he and his father maintained a close relationship. After his father passed, Jason told me he wanted children. He wanted that same relationship with a son.

In September of 2002, we went to New Orleans with a group of friends to watch Texas play Tulane in the Superdome. We stayed at the Soniat House hotel in the French Quarter and six weeks later, I learned that I was pregnant. I prayed it was a son. I wanted that for Jason.

As much as we were overjoyed, Elizabeth was ecstatic. She took us to the Four Seasons in Nevis that spring. Quite pregnant, I literally bumped into Kelly Ripa, who was there with her husband and children. I took in the luxury, the beauty of the place, and the scene with gratitude. I was so incredibly blessed to have married into this family and to experience all of this.

Elizabeth was so excited about having a grandchild that she invited me to Chicago to stay at the Peninsula Hotel and shop for the nursery. We went to a luxury baby boutique where she purchased a crib, custom bedding, matching curtains, a nursing chair, and a high-end stroller. Then she took me to Neiman Marcus, where she purchased outfits for every phase of the first year of our son's life. She hosted a baby shower for me at her home in Michigan. After the baby shower, she confided in me that she had been having some health issues and that she would be going in for a heart valve replacement at the Mayo Clinic in Rochester, Minnesota, a few weeks before my due date. She told me that it was a fairly routine procedure and not to worry—that she fully expected to be recovered in time to come help after the baby was born.

Elizabeth went in for her surgery and the surgeon decided to repair her heart valve instead of replacing it. We were told that all was well and that Elizabeth was recovering nicely, but about a week later we were informed that the valve repair had failed, and that Elizabeth was being transported back to the Mayo Clinic for further emergency surgery. We were now about a week from my due date. Jason was conflicted—did he stay with his pregnant wife or rush to his mother's bedside? It was a cruel choice. Jason stayed with me, and our son, Tommy, was born on June 15, 2003. Nine days later, Elizabeth passed away, on Heather's birthday, June 24. My husband had lost both of his parents in a year's time. He was devastated.

I tried to comfort him as I navigated new motherhood, learning how to breastfeed, and the like. Tommy was too young for vaccinations, so we consulted our pediatrician about possible travel, and he advised that we should drive to Michigan for the funeral.

Jason came from a very wealthy family. His grandfather was the EVP of sales at a Fortune 500 company. He took the money he made there and invested in real estate, buying up huge swaths of land. Money was placed in trust for his children and grandchildren. When Jason's grandmother passed away in 1998, her estate was valued in the tens of millions. As long as I had known Elizabeth, she was regularly and consistently telling her kids that what she had would soon be theirs. She had recently purchased a beautiful home on the intercoastal waterway in Fort Lauderdale, which she gutted and remodeled, sparing no expense. We visited there a few times before she passed. Each time, she told Jason and Heather that this home would be part of their inheritance.

At the funeral, Elizabeth's stockbroker—whom I had met on a previous trip and had observed having hushed conversations with Elizabeth's husband, Harold—approached me. "No need to worry about Harold!" she said as she flipped her bad hair extensions. "He's all taken care of!" I tried to make sense of her words— why would I be worried about Harold? Harold was Elizabeth's scotch-drinking, cigarette-smoking husband. He had a job, but his lifestyle was all because of Elizabeth. It was clear to me that Harold resented Elizabeth. There was no love or affection between them. Harold would escape to the "hardware" store for hours on a daily basis. This was laughable because Harold did not know a hammer from a screwdriver. To be fair, he had put up with a lot, having been married to her through the depths of her alcoholism. He stayed married to her for the perks, and now he felt entitled. I knew he was passive-aggressive, but we all underestimated him. At the funeral, we learned that the will Harold claimed was Elizabeth's last will and testament left everything—EVERYTHING—to Harold. Jason and Heather *were not even mentioned in the will.* Now I understood the stockbroker's comment. Was she in on this? Our heads were spinning. It made no sense. None. This was not what Elizabeth intended, I was sure of that. My husband had lost his father and mother in the period of a year, and now this???

We hired an attorney, but the Michigan Supreme Court had recently issued an opinion that severely limited our ability to contest the will. Harold settled with each child, but they received nothing compared to what they had been promised. I will give credit to Jason that, as upsetting as all of this was, he just wanted his mom back. He had ten great years with her sober and loved her dearly. As I tried to comfort my husband, I wallowed in my own grief. I had only a few years with Elizabeth. She was the mother I had always wanted. She doted on me and we genuinely enjoyed each other's company. I was also immensely sad for Tommy. His grandmother loved him so much, but he would never know her.

My book group stepped in, bringing meals, flowers, notes of condolence, and gifts for Tommy. I leaned on them for advice on being a new mom. My friends were my family and source of support. The year 2003 wasn't done with us yet—my maternal grandmother, an uncle, and a friend passed away. I referred to 2003 as Four Funerals and a Wedding, as it was the year my cousin married.

We focused on our son and continued to remodel our house, trying to move past the pain of so much loss. We decided to have another child, and Andy was born in March of 2005. As I breast-fed Andy, Jason would take Tommy a lot of the time. Jason, who is fiercely logical, could not comprehend the behavior of a toddler. He would grow frustrated and sometimes say things that were inappropriate. I could tell that my husband was struggling. He was depressed and angry at the world. I called my therapist and got a recommendation from her for an excellent therapist for men.

Thankfully, with Heather's support, we were able to get Jason to start therapy. My therapist warned me that things might get worse before they got better. Depression is anger turned inward.

Therapy helped Jason's depression as he learned to articulate his feelings. However, the anger he had been internalizing was often now directed at me. He was quick to lash out verbally and was hypercritical of me and the kids.

In 1998, my sister went on a cruise with her boyfriend around the same time that I had gone on the Alaskan cruise with Jason. My sister and her boyfriend broke up and Jason and I got engaged. My sister stopped speaking to me. She did not attend my wedding to Jason or acknowledge the births of my sons. In 2007, after nine years of not speaking to me, my sister announced that she was engaged and invited me to attend her wedding in Irvine, California. Jason hated my sister because he saw the pain her actions caused. He declared that he would not be attending and asked me repeatedly why I would go after she had not attended our wedding. She was my sister. I wanted to heal the relationship, so I accepted the invitation and asked if my best friend from high school, whom Tiffany knew well, could attend in Jason's place. She agreed.

My sister married Allan Oakley Hunter, Jr., the son of a United States congressman, and the former chairman of Fannie Mae. Allan, Jr. was successful in his own right, having founded and sold two companies. Along with his business partner, Scott Ingraham, Allan founded Oasis Residential, which was sold to Camden Property Trust for $392 million in 1998. They later founded Rent.com, which they sold to eBay for $415 million in 2004. Allan had survived throat cancer and was ready to enjoy the fruits of his labor. They were married at Shady Canyon Country Club under an arch of roses on a picture-perfect day, surrounded by scions of business. Allan whisked her off to a monthlong honeymoon in Europe. Then, they settled into their $13 million home in Shady Canyon, next door to tennis star Lindsay Davenport and across the canyon from baseball great Mark McGuire. My sister was living a fairy tale. I later learned that my sister had been pregnant at her wedding—tall and thin, she disguised it even from me. On September 21, 2007, Tiffany gave birth to Lucy Grace Hunter. I spoke to her on the phone, and she was ecstatic. She had never been so happy. Her dreams had come true.

The next day, Jason called me on his way into work; he had been listening to Howard Stern, who covered the local New York news on his show. The show had covered a story about Trey Hunter, Allan's son from a previous marriage, who was a freshman at NYU. According to the show, Trey had jumped off the roof of his dormitory and killed himself within hours of learning about the birth of his baby sister. The *New York Post* picked up the story, "Lovesick Teen Death Leap," detailing the circumstances of his death. My head was spinning. None of this made any sense. I picked up the phone and called my sister. I was met with cries of anguish and sorrow. "Trey is dead! Trey is dead! How could this happen?" I realized in that moment that my sister needed me. Our mother was in an assisted living facility. Tiffany was new to Orange County, having relocated there from La Jolla to marry Allan. She didn't have girlfriends nearby to support her. I hopped on a plane and flew to Orange County. When I arrived, I took Lucy from her arms to feed her so that she could be there for Allan, who now had to deal with the death of his son eclipsing the birth of his daughter. And sadly, I understood better than anyone what it felt like to have your child's joyous birth be eclipsed by the death of a loved one.

Around this time, Jason was laid off from his job at a local technology company. He had plenty of money and I was working, so I wasn't that concerned. Determined to be supportive of him in light of all he had been through, I left him alone. After a month of him doing nothing, not even working out, I asked him what his plan was. He said that he didn't have one. This frustrated me. He had long talked about getting into the home audio/video business and I encouraged him to do so. Jason partnered with the brother of a friend and when I met with lawyers, I would tell them about his new business. Lawyers were his perfect customers. They wanted the status of an expensive and sophisticated home audio/video system, but they couldn't be bothered to install it themselves. Most of Jason's work was done after typical business hours and over weekends. This meant that in addition to completing my own work, I was watching the kids all the time after work, but I did it gladly—I wanted to see his business succeed.

After a few months of this, I noticed that Jason was drinking every night. Given his family history, this really alarmed me. I approached him one night to talk and find out what was bothering him. "You treat me like a shitbox," he said. What? Were we in alternate realities? I was doing everything in my power to be supportive of him. After probing him further, I learned that he resented my involvement in his business. OK, got it. Message received. He resented my support. This was an illuminating moment for me. I had been giving and giving and giving and getting nothing in return. I was done. "You are on your own," I said. "I won't have anything to do with your business anymore." Within a few months, he shut down his business.

Early in 2009, after Jason shut down his business, I asked him again what the plan was. When we were dating, he told me a story about when he moved to Austin in the early 1990s. Jobs were scarce back then, and he took a job delivering pizzas for Pizza Hut and volunteered at the Capital Area Food Bank while he was looking for other work. After my experience with Beaux, a strong work ethic became very important to me, so Jason's work history convinced me that no matter how bad things got, he would always work and be a provider. Now, I was feeling betrayed and misled. "So, what is plan B?" I asked him. Jason was lying on the couch with the remote in hand as the nanny, who we were paying for with my salary, was watching our children so that I could work. Jason wasn't taking care of himself. He wasn't helping with the kids. He wasn't looking for another job. Jason replied, "Plan B is that you are going to work harder." This was another one of those light-switch moments. This was the moment that our marriage died.

As I absorbed his words, I flashed back to being told by my father that my life wasn't worth fifty dollars, to being told in the hospital that "he wasn't paying for it." How did I end up here again? I'm not worthy of being supported? His words exploded in my heart and cut me to my soul. As my emotions churned, my legal background came into focus. Like a wave that washed over me, I realized how foolish I had been. Jason had always promised that his trust fund and inheritance would be our retirement fund, so we spent the money that I made and didn't use it for savings. I realized in that moment that his wealth was his separate property and that my business profits were community property. I was fucked. He could literally lie there on the couch, remote in hand, for the rest of his life, and not work another day. I felt betrayed. I had given him thirteen years of my life and two children. I knew that day that it was over. I was alone in my marriage but determined to keep it intact for my boys.

Day by day I died a little more. Jason had gained a lot of weight since we were married. He was drinking more and regularly making snide, cutting remarks. Then, a month later, I met someone. A very handsome, successful guy who expressed a genuine interest in me. We would talk on the phone for hours on end. It was refreshing to have someone genuinely want to know about me and my thoughts and feelings. I realized that my relationship with Jason, much like my relationship with my father, was all about him. It didn't start out that way, but with everything that had happened to us, it's where we ended up. This was a familiar pattern for me—put everyone else first—but I got lost in the process. And this new guy was a reminder that I existed outside of this relationship. It was as if I was dying of thirst and this guy offered me a sip of water—and I reached for the whole glass.

Jason will say that the affair is what ended our marriage. It wasn't. I felt like I was dying in our marriage. I needed to escape it. My therapist characterized my behavior as an "exit affair." I saw our marriage as already over and my affair was the escape mechanism.

While understandable given his anger and pain, Jason had become sarcastic and critical. Not only did he not compliment me, but he was also constantly making digs at me, pointing out my flaws, just as my father had, and it was killing me.

The affair was brief, and I deeply regret hurting Jason, but it brought closure. And while I felt societal pressure to try to keep the family together for the boys, I knew in my heart that divorce was the best thing for all of us. Jason was experiencing so much mental pain and anger from the cards that life had dealt him. I knew that he needed a break from all of us. We were all drowning. One of us had to reach for a life raft to save the family.

The divorce rocked our friend group because no one saw it coming. I never spoke ill of Jason. I kept rearranging the deck chairs on the Titanic, proclaiming the glory of the ship until it crashed into the iceberg and survival mechanisms kicked in. One of the hardest things for me was waking up and realizing that the luxury liner I was on had cracks in the hull. I had to take my blinders off and look at my marriage objectively. Those light-switch moments had that jarring effect.

As much as I needed to escape my marriage to survive, it was of utmost importance to me HOW I handled the divorce. Jason had told me that he felt like his mother had handicapped his relationship with his father. I did not want that to happen with our boys. I knew how critical it was for them to have a strong relationship with their father. It was in that spirit that I approached the divorce. I used to joke that Jason's money was the third person in our marriage, it was so important to him. I knew this was his touchstone. I knew that one can't put a price on peace and elected to walk away with half of the proceeds of the house and my business. We were divorced on the sixtieth day after the waiting period—everything had been agreed to. I hung photos of Jason in the boys' rooms, and more than not speaking ill of him, I spoke glowingly of his good qualities.

After my divorce, I took the boys to spend Christmas with my sister. After we left, Allan became infected with H1N1. Tiffany urged him to go to the hospital, but he was depressed and didn't want to go. By the time she got him to the hospital, his pulse oxygen was so low that the doctors induced a coma and put him on a ventilator. Allan was in a coma for a month. My sister was at his bedside. When he came out of the coma, the doctors discovered that the radiation for his earlier throat cancer and the long period of intubation before a trach was put in had caused so much scarring in his throat and mouth that he had developed lockjaw. In addition, anything that went into his mouth went directly into his lungs. He would never be able to eat or drink again. He was left with a permanent feeding tube. In spite of this, my sister remained at Allan's side. She was just happy to have her husband back.

In June of 2011, my brother, Todd, hosted Tiffany and me and our children at his vacation home in Wildwood, New Jersey. Allan did not accompany Tiffany on the trip. Tiffany confided in me that Allan had been acting erratically and she had discovered that he had been buying pain pills in bulk, grinding them up, and putting them through his feeding tube. He had been in several car accidents, which my sister suspected were a result of the drugs. Also, his mood had changed from gratitude for my sister to being moody and distant.

At the conclusion of our vacation, Tiffany received an email from Allan copying sixteen people and saying that he had moved out and wanted a divorce. Tiffany was stunned. She was by his side through so much drama and tragedy. Yet, she still loved him in spite of it all.

Tiffany returned to their Shady Canyon home and true to his word, Allan was gone. She didn't hear from him for a couple of months until she was served divorce papers. Only then did she learn that he had moved into the Villas at the Resort at Pelican Hill, next door to Kobe Bryant, who was separated from his wife at that time.

What ensued was a divorce of epic proportions. Allan was now directing all of his rage about losing his son, landing in a coma, and the long-term health consequences at my sister. He demanded joint custody of their daughter, whom he largely ignored. While many issues were covered by their prenuptial agreement, custody and child support were not. Allan changed lawyers five times, finally landing on Stephen Kolodny, a famously ruthless, cruel bulldog. My sister hired Trope and Trope, the white knights of Hollywood divorce attorneys. In total, they spent $3 million on their divorce. Most of that paid to Steve Kolodny to make my sister suffer.

I describe my sister's marriage to Allan as a "fairy tale gone wrong." Behind the beautiful trappings of their life were narcissism, physical and mental illness, and pain. As they say, "marry a rich man and you'll earn every penny." My sister paid with her suffering. More than being tossed aside, Allan made her suffering his mission.

Through it all, I watched my sister fight for her daughter and scramble to keep her head above water. She moved from the Shady Canyon house to a modest home in Huntington Beach. She channeled her energy into launching an interior design business, Tiffany Hunter Home.

My life story and family history are littered with fortunes made and lost. I've witnessed pain, suffering, resentment, deceit, mental illness, drug addiction, and suicide all flowing from an obsession with money. I used to cry that it was unfair that I didn't get the same treatment as my brother or sister. Given my family history, I resented the fact that I hadn't inherited a dime from anyone. I was initially jealous of my sister and her storybook life. But over time, I have come to realize that none of this bullshit matters. I've got me and I'm all I need to take care of me. I'm in charge of my own happiness. Because I wasn't given anything, I don't owe anyone anything. I'm free. Totally free to choose my own path and be my authentic self. The only limitations are the ones that I set for myself. I can take care of myself. I have stopped expecting things from the people in my life. Without expectation, there is no possibility for disappointment. Instead of focusing outwardly on what others can or should do for me, I look inward to what I can do for myself and others. When someone shows up, gives, or supports, I experience genuine gratitude. Their action is not simply an expectation met, rather it is a gift to be cherished.

As for men, I have personally witnessed and experienced what it is like to be with a man who loves his money more than anything else. It's toxic, destructive, and painful.

My friend Henry, who is a serial entrepreneur and the most networked guy I know, said he wanted to set me up. "What kind of guys do you like to date?" he asked. I replied, "I want a man who can love me more than money." To which he replied, "Well, that knocks out 95 percent of them!" But that is the bar that I have set. Our family legacy of pain, resentment, and destruction around the love of money ends here. What a gift to have this clarity! The lesson has been learned. It's not the money that is the problem—it's the love of it. It has been said that "the love of money is the root of all evil." I know this to be true, so I'm holding out for that man who loves me more than money. I have learned that I am worthy of both money and love as I am today, without twisting or contorting myself to please anyone.

CHAPTER SEVEN

DIVORCE

"I used to hope that you would bring me
flowers. Now I plant my own."

—RACHEL WOLCHIN

Having been twice divorced, I can tell you that divorce is something so painful that I wouldn't wish it on my worst enemy. That being said, I am certain that both of my divorces were 100 percent the right decision. With my first husband, I never should have married him in the first place. We were not meant to be together. With Jason, my second husband, I loved him dearly, but love isn't enough to sustain a relationship. Women need to trust, admire, and respect their partner and once those things are gone, the relationship is dead. They also need equal investment. One party can't be the only one "watering the plants." Both parties need to be regularly watering and fertilizing the relationship to keep it alive.

During my second divorce, while I was in absolute agony, a good friend said to me, "You may not want to hear this now, but with adversity comes opportunity." She was right. I didn't want to hear it. But her words stayed with me, and I started to consider what she said. My divorce gave me freedom. Suddenly, I had a clean slate. I was free of living my life to keep him happy. The heavy criticism I faced from my friends, while indescribably painful, pushed me outside their circle and unshackled me from keeping up with the Joneses. I was suddenly free from the cages of my relationship, society, and the expectations of others. I had the opportunity to design a life that made me happy and that brought me joy. Divorce is the death of a marriage, but it is also the birth of a new life full of opportunity.

Divorce equaled rejection from family and friends, but this also meant freedom. After living my entire life trying to please others, I was thrust into discovering what would make me happy and how I wanted to live my life.

One of my first dates after my second divorce was with a handsome, debonair lawyer in Dallas. He took me to dinner at Rosewood Mansion on Turtle Creek. It was a fabulous dinner. As he drove me back to my hotel in his throaty Mercedes SL 500 convertible, he asked me what kind of music I liked and what were my favorite restaurants in Austin? I was totally stumped. I couldn't name a single band. I couldn't list a restaurant. We always listened to *Jason's* music and went where *he* liked to eat. I had no opinion. None. It was in that moment that I realized that I had become my mother. It was clear that I had a lot of work to do. I needed to figure out what I liked, what I needed, and who I was. I needed to stand on my own. It was critical that I discover who I was before I could be in a relationship with someone else.

I started questioning everything—religion, political affiliations, fashion, lifestyle choices. Who was I? What did I stand for? As I tried to figure these things out, I was like a wobbly fawn, careening into objects, often falling down. As the first in my group of friends to get divorced, there was no one to comfort me. All my attempts at being true to myself were met with criticism and shaming. But there was an important lesson in this: as I wished for grace, I committed to offering grace to others. I'll admit I used to be very judgmental of others. But divorce ripped the scales from my eyes; it taught me to hold space open for others. Gradually, as my friends began to get divorced, they came to me and I was able to listen to them without judgment. I knew that they might engage in bizarre and uncharacteristic behavior because they were trying to find their way, just like I had. I was able to offer them unconditional love and support. As more and more women began to confide in me, I learned that the more perfect the facade, the more likely that there was some serious drama behind the scenes. *People who are authentic don't have to be perfect.* I also learned that "perfect" people are often the most judgmental. They look for the flaws in others to make themselves feel better.

As women began to confide in me some of their deepest, darkest secrets, I realized that I loved these women even more for being real with me. I learned to stop judging people in general. I realized that everyone has a story. We have no idea what people have been through, what has shaped them. My capacity for empathy expanded exponentially.

I set about exploring who I was and what mattered to me. I realized that while I was married, I had even begun to dress like my mother. I went through my closet and got rid of all of my Lilly Pulitzer dresses, flats, and cardigans. I went shopping at a local boutique, Estilo, where the owner, Stephanie, and store manager, Erin, helped to guide me toward items that flattered my figure, reflected my personality, and didn't scream "mom." When discussing politics or religion, I would stop and ask myself: *do I really believe this or am I simply parroting my parents?* I continued therapy, read self-help books, sought to expand my circle of friends. I explored new restaurants and traveled to new places. I was determined to become a complete individual—not the other half of a couple or an acolyte of my father. Over time as I grew to learn more about myself, I curated my own playlist and never looked back.

As proof that I've done the work, here is a list of my favorite restaurants in Austin:

Aba, ATX Cocina, Bob's rooftop, Clark's, Group Therapy, Josephine House, Justine's, Lambert's, Lenoir, Lin's Asian, Peacock, Red Ash, Salt Lick, Summer House, Sway, Uchi, Uchiko, Vespaio, Zanzibar.

I've discovered the music that I love—so much so that I created a playlist for this book. It can be found on Spotify; search for Carrington Smith and select the playlist "Blooming: I'd rather be me."

CHAPTER EIGHT

CAREER

*"In order to be irreplaceable, one
must always be different."*

—COCO CHANEL

I entered Tulane Law School in August of 1990 during the savings and loan crisis. From 1986 to 1995, 1,043 of the 3,234 savings and loan associations (S&Ls) in the United States failed, causing major financial upheaval. Accompanied by upheaval in the oil and gas market and a slew of bankruptcies, the job market for lawyers in the early 1990s could be described in one word: terrible.

I finished my first year of law school in the top 20 percent of my class, but without a slot on the law review journal, I was not invited to interview with the few firms that came on campus that year. This was before the widespread use of email, so most of our law school class hired résumé services to mail their résumés to the top 200 firms in the United States. I was skeptical of this "shotgun" approach but desperate for a job; I could not take an unpaid clerkship. I needed the money. I watched as my classmates scrambled; collectively, they all targeted the same firms and used the same approach—with little success. I needed to do something to stand out from the crowd. I had to find a paying job, and that desperation led to contemplation and strategic thinking. First, I thought about which firms were hiring. Which practice areas were growing? I looked at smaller markets and settled on Atlanta. At the time, Atlanta was the fastest-growing city in the United States. Companies were moving there on a regular basis. Finally, I looked at my network. Who did I know who could make an introduction for me to one of the firms that I had identified? Then, I wrote *one* letter to the managing partner of the firm. The letter communicated my knowledge about the firm, our connection in common, why I wanted to work there, and what I had to give. More specifically, why they should hire me. The firm was Neely & Player, a local midsized firm with a thriving national insurance defense practice.[1] The letter was addressed to Ned Neely. He picked up the phone and called me when he received my letter! My targeted approach had landed me a job! Adversity had borne creativity.

With my ear surgeries, hospitalization during finals, and financial and other struggles, I ended up finishing law school in the middle of my class. More than any other profession, lawyers are grade snobs. They ask for your transcripts and class standing each time you apply for a job and your grades follow you for the rest of

---

1 Neely was also known for representing Rob Lowe in the civil lawsuit filed by the mother of a teenage girl who was videotaped having sex with Lowe during the Democratic Convention held in Atlanta in 1988.

your career. I'm not aware of another profession where your success in school is so determinative of your success in the profession. Graduating from law school, I faced not only a horrible job market, but I had handicapped the likelihood of my success by not graduating at the top of my class. Add to this equation that I had married a bar manager from Bourbon Street—my prospects were not good.

We moved to Austin, and I registered for the Texas Bar Exam. I worked at the Oasis Restaurant as a hostess while I studied for the exam and looked for work. I reached out to The University of Texas School of Law Career Services office and subscribed to their job bulletin. The only job advertised that summer in Austin was at a law firm that specialized in property tax. I went to law school to avoid anything math related, but I was desperate, so I applied.

A few weeks later, I received a phone call from one of the partners. He told me that he had received over 300 resumes. The job ad specified that they were looking for an Associate/Client Liaison. About 250 of those who applied did not address the client liaison aspect of the job; of those who had, they selected ten finalists. They were asking each of the ten finalists to write them a letter explaining why they should hire them.

A few months earlier, I was on a Southwest Airlines flight from New Orleans to Austin and I sat next to Carole Keeton Rylander (now Strayhorn), the former mayor of Austin. I recognized her and struck up a conversation. At the end of our flight, Carol gave me her business card. "If you ever need anything, please feel free to call me," she said. I tucked away her card for safekeeping. Dusting off her card, I attached it to my letter to the firm. "Why hire me?" I wrote. "Ask Carol Keeton Rylander." I went onto explain how I had met her and immediately established rapport. I explained how these were exactly the skills that they were looking for in a client liaison. The managing partner called me and said, "You got my attention. Let's meet." I got the job.

I was so excited. My first job as an attorney! While I dreaded the subject matter, at least it was litigation. I quickly learned that while there was little that was sexy about property tax, very few attorneys practiced in this area, so it was easy to establish yourself as an expert. The partners wanted a client liaison because they liked practicing law but hated dealing with the clients. This presented a huge opportunity for me. Our clients were mostly Fortune 500 companies, banks, and REITs. I had immediate and continuous exposure to our clients and established some great relationships.

But this job had a dark side—the firm was highly dysfunctional. One of the staff members was sleeping with one of the partners, there were substance abuse issues, the partners fought constantly, and there was a hostile work environment. A former Texas Supreme Court justice served as Of Counsel to the firm, and he was notorious for his sexual harassment. "Red Rover, Red Rover, please bend over," he would say to me. "My, oh my, your breasts look lovely in that blouse!" he said. I sought out legal advice from an employment lawyer and learned that the laws against sexual discrimination only applied to companies with fifteen or more employees. Our firm had fourteen employees. Now, I understood why this former Texas Supreme Court justice had affiliated with our firm and not an AMLAW 100 firm—he could do as he wished.

The firm was toxic. My only option was to leave. As I prepared my résumé, I asked a client if I could use him for a reference. The client was the former First City Bank of Texas. Like many other banks, the bank was going through liquidation. Jerry Thompson was one of the few executives left and in charge of overseeing all of the legal matters. Jerry responded, "Carrie, I'm currently dealing with over 400 different lawyers at some of the best firms in the country. You are the only one who asks me how I'm doing. You are the only one who took me to lunch on my birthday. You deliver great client service and get us great results. I can give you a reference. But wherever you go, we're going with you. And I have sixteen more cases for you." I was speechless. This was a totally unexpected turn of events. I was a second-year associate and suddenly I had portable business. I was immensely flattered but unsure of what to do.

I consulted with the two other associates at the firm who were much more senior than I. What should I do? We were all fed up with the craziness at the firm. I could use their expertise to try cases, so we decided to form our own firm. If they were going to allow me to be sexually harassed, I would vote with my feet. We cleaned out our offices in the middle of the night, and the next morning our new firm was launched. Word spread around the local legal community about the firm that had lost all of its associates in the middle of the night. People cheered us on. We had the courage to do what so many mistreated associates had dreamed of. As a second-year lawyer, I was suddenly a business owner and entirely responsible for generating my own income. I was excited and terrified all at once.

I learned a lot from this experience. I brought in the majority of the firm's business and did about half of the work, but the profits were split equally. One of the partners was focused on administrative matters and was not producing. The other partner had an expansive network but could not bring himself to ask for business. We had too much overhead—office space, employees, office equipment. Our firm was dysfunctional in its own way. I was miserable and frustrated. I could not get my partners to change their behavior or our compensation structure. We were in business for two years when I was approached by a headhunter to change firms. I could double my income and leave the headaches behind. I was in.

First, I needed to extricate myself from my former firm, and we had a lot of debt. Jason and I were dating at this point, and I was still struggling to pay off my student loans. He stepped in and gave me $20,000 to cash out of my former firm. I was incredibly grateful to him.

I settled in at my new firm. I had been practicing law for five years and my star in the property tax area was rising. I got a phone call one day from Michael Biggs, Head of Asset Management at Camden Property Trust. They were set for trial in sixty days in Travis County and he wanted to fire his current attorneys and hire me to try the case. Was he crazy? His current attorneys wanted him to settle the case, but he wanted to take it to trial. I had never tried a case before, I told him. He had heard good things about me, and he was willing to take that risk. I made sure that he understood that the likelihood of success was low but with that understanding, I agreed to take the case. Maybe I was the one who was crazy!

Up until that time, all property tax trials were formulaic. Each side would hire an appraiser to write a report offering an opinion of value of the property in question and the trial would be a battle of the experts. I quickly learned that this case had not settled because our expert had based his opinion of value on one sale—and he had the wrong sales price. Getting the case at sixty days out, there was no time to hire another appraiser and get another report. We were stuck with our expert. The attorney on the other side had never lost a case. This case looked like a loser and by hiring an attorney who had never tried a case, everyone thought there was no chance that we could win.

Everyone. Including the partners at my firm. They had a trial for Chevron in Houston that same week. They were too busy to help me, they said. I knew that they were distancing themselves because they believed that I would lose. Begrudgingly, they agreed to send one partner to monitor the litigation, but I was on my own to try the case. Their lack of confidence in me and in the outcome shook me, but I was determined and the client's confidence in me was unwavering.

The expert report was a massive obstacle. How could I fix this problem? All eyes were on me. Time to get creative. The litigation was about the value of an apartment complex in the north area of Austin, so I designated the number one commercial real estate broker for apartment sales in the Austin area as an additional expert. The other side's appraiser arrived at his value for the apartment complex using sales in the north*west* area of Austin, arriving at a higher value. I put the commercial real estate broker on the stand. "Mr. Sorrell, what is the most important rule of real estate?" I asked. "Location, location, location," he responded. Then, he explained how values in the more desirable area of Northwest Austin were higher than in North Austin, where the property was located. He was able to walk through each relevant sale and offer his own opinion of value. While not exotic, what I had done was outside the norm. The very way that I was trying my case and putting on evidence was unexpected—and this left my opponent scrambling.

Buzz began to build. Word got out. She might actually win this trial. Each day more people came to watch. Then, after a five-day bench trial, Judge Pete Lowry ruled in our favor, setting the value at our number. We had won! As I was packing up my things, the bailiff approached me. He leaned in and whispered, tilting his head toward the judge, "You had him at hello! Great work, young lady."

While I was initially angry that the partners had abandoned me and given me zero support for the trial, the credit was mine alone—I had tried the case entirely on my own. No one could take that from me. Confronted with what was perceived by most as an insurmountable obstacle, I learned that hard work, extensive preparation, strategic thinking, creativity, and determination carved a path to victory. *The impossible became possible with a shift in perspective and a belief in myself.*

The partners sent me a bottle of Dom Pérignon to celebrate the win. I reached out to my friends, looking to celebrate—but I had been preparing for trial and in trial for over sixty days and they had forgotten about me. As exhilarating as the win was, this was a lonely life that I had chosen. I did a few more trials but grew increasingly dissatisfied with the lifestyle of a litigator. I served on the board of directors of the Austin Bar Association and loved working and socializing with other lawyers. I enjoyed client development and was great at keeping clients happy. But I was still paying off my enormous law school loans; was there a way to still use my law degree and find a career that made me happy?

I started to think about my experience with the headhunter and wondered if that might present a better life for me. I read *What Color Is Your Parachute?* and did some self-assessments. I thought about the kind of life that I wished to lead. What would a typical day look like? How would I be spending my time and with whom?

After concluding that legal headhunting was what I wished to pursue, I acted with clarity and courage. There were no openings at the existing shops in Austin, so I reached out to some national recruiting firms and pitched opening an Austin office. I had researched the market and knew where the opportunities were. I talked about my extensive network and client development skills. After my second pitch, the hiring manager said, "You closed me in the first five minutes of our call. I have to hire you before someone else does." Yeeesssss!!! I had my foot in the door! I was so excited to launch my new career. I couldn't wait to tell the partners, "Hasta la vista!"

The one thing that I did not research? The recruiting firm that I was joining. Gulp. They were a disaster. I made a placement within two weeks of starting at the firm—a company record. I was ecstatic. I immediately loved the industry, but my company was offering very little support or supervision. I wanted to be great at this but there were few resources and no mentors. Here I was again wringing my hands, frustrated by a poorly run business. There was a pattern here. The universe was sending me a message and I just wasn't getting it.

In December of 2000, I announced that I would be leaving the company and starting my own firm. Just in time for the internet bubble to burst. The booming economy in Austin disappeared so fast that Intel, which was building its headquarters in downtown Austin, abandoned the building midconstruction. The half-finished skeleton of that building stood as a memorial to what once was until it was demolished in 2007 and replaced with a new federal courthouse.

What then? I had started my own business and there was no business to get! How would I survive, let alone thrive? I sat back and reflected. I didn't panic. I faced the impending economic disaster with open eyes and strategic vision. There had to be opportunity in here somewhere.

During the economic boom, a number of California law firms had opened Austin offices. These firms were focused on serving technology companies and had been growing like gangbusters. They leased entire office buildings with luxury buildouts to house hundreds of lawyers. Most every legal recruiter in Texas was focused on placing attorneys with these firms. They were all chasing the same thing. I quickly realized that the more conventional, old-guard firms in Austin were being ignored by these same recruiters. By swimming in the opposite direction of the crowd, I found opportunity. And when the tech bubble burst and the California firms imploded, I had solid relationships and a strong track record with these firms, so they returned to me. Their business was less impacted because it was more diverse and less tech-focused. I suddenly had business when others did not. I watched many of my competitors exit the industry or go out of business.

I had some work, but it wasn't enough. I needed a strategy. I asked myself, "What do lawyers most want that is not available to them?" My answer: in-house jobs. The in-house legal job—a job working directly for a company, as opposed to a law firm—has been idolized by countless lawyers as the holy grail of legal jobs. The problem in 2001 was that there was no resource for identifying the people who held these jobs or the opportunities themselves. LinkedIn did not yet exist. I spent the next few months researching and identifying every in-house lawyer in Austin—400 total. As I reached out to these lawyers, I quickly learned that there was no association or group in Austin that served them. At the time, I was serving on the board of the Austin Bar Association and with the massive retraction in the economy, they were looking for new revenue opportunities. How could we get more lawyers to join? I proposed starting a section to serve the in-house lawyers. Our president responded, "I love the idea. And you are in charge of the new section!"

I was the fox guarding the henhouse, but I knew *how* I ramped up this section would be critical to my business's success. I reached out to in-house lawyers that I knew and asked them to serve as the officers for the section and I acted as the administrator. I planned events, got speakers, and marketed the events. I approached the section with the attitude of service. I was there to help, not to sell. I established deep friendships with many in this group and it was so successful that the Association of Corporate Counsel eventually decided to open an Austin chapter and our group was merged into theirs. In the midst of all of this, September 11 happened. What we thought was bad got much, much worse. Instead of getting paralyzed by the shitstorm around me, I stayed focused on my plan. I planted seeds. I gave. I served. And then my business took off.

CHAPTER NINE

STEPPING INTO THE LIGHT

"You were not born to fit in.
You were born to stand out."

—RUPAUL

During the time that I was in law school at Tulane University in New Orleans, my brother became engaged to a woman who was from Baton Rouge, Louisiana. As the wedding approached, my maternal grandmother, Mimi, asked that I organize a day-after brunch in New Orleans for our family members who planned on attending. I surveyed the local restaurants and, given the large size of our group—about twelve people—I made a reservation at the Court of Two Sisters. I thought that their jazz brunch would be a great way to showcase New Orleans and finish off the weekend.

My sister was staying with me at my apartment in New Orleans. The day of the wedding, we drove to Baton Rouge to attend the ceremony and reception. We spent the night in Baton Rouge but returned to my apartment the following day to freshen up before the brunch. My sister was in a mood. Our new sister-in-law, Lee, had not invited us to be bridesmaids, but instead had relegated us to being cake servers. We were both smarting from our lack of importance in the wedding. Tiffany was really struggling. She was usually the center of attention, so to be so thoroughly sidelined— and then have the focus on Todd and Lee—really irked her. This day, I was the focus of attention since I was the one who organized the brunch.

When we arrived back at my apartment, we had about two hours before the brunch—plenty of time to get ready and get there on time. Tiffany was moving slowly. Very slowly. Very, very slowly.

"Tiffany, if we don't get going, we are going to be late. We need to get there before everyone else so I can direct everyone to our table. Mimi asked me to be there early," I implored.

"I need to iron my shirt," Tiffany replied, as she proceeded to borrow my ironing board and iron. I watched the clock and began to pace as my sister very, very slowly and deliberately moved the iron on her shirt. She curled her hair some more. She retouched her makeup. She was purposefully stalling to make us late.

"Tiffany, we need to go NOW!" I said as I watched the clock tick. If we left then, we might get there on time. Getting there early was no longer going to happen. Arriving on time was starting to look like history. My sister replied in a haughty voice, "You HAVE to wait for me, because YOU are taking me." I watched the clock tick further. I could feel Mimi's wrath. She was going to be furious.

Being late was a sign of disrespect. I was being set up by my sister.

I found the phone book and flipped to the yellow pages for taxi companies (ride-sharing did not yet exist). This was New Orleans. There were taxis everywhere. I put some cash on the counter. "I'm leaving. I need to get there. You can come with me now or call yourself a taxi."

"YOU. MUST. WAIT FOR ME!!!!" Tiffany commanded as she continued to move in deliberately and ridiculously slow motion. "You HAVE to wait for me, and YOU have to take me!!!"

Furious at my sister and fearing Mimi's wrath, I replied, "I'm leaving now. Call yourself a taxi!" And I walked out the door.

When I arrived at the restaurant, everyone was waiting for me. True to form, Mimi was furious with me. She berated me in front of all of my family members for being late: "You are so rude and disrespectful! I ask you to do ONE thing, and you can't make it here on time!" I was embarrassed and humiliated. After I showed the group to our table and helped Mimi through the buffet line, I realized that my father was no longer with the group. "Where's Dad?" I asked my mom. "He went to go pick up your sister!" my mother replied angrily. "What? I told her to call a taxi!" I said. "Well, she called the restaurant and had the maître d' come find your dad, and now he's not here because he is picking up Tiffany," she said in a tone of annoyance.

Boy, my sister is a piece of work, I thought to myself, feeling a pit growing in my stomach. I tried to engage in conversation with my relatives and enjoy the brunch as best I could. Suddenly, I saw my father out of the corner of my eye; he scowled at me and gave me a look of total disgust. The next thing I knew, my sister appeared next to me. She grabbed a glass of water and a knife and began to clink the glass to get everyone's attention. She was doing it so loudly that not only did she get the attention of our group, but nearly everyone in the restaurant was staring at my sister. She stood behind me, holding the glass of water over my head. "I want everyone here to know what a total BITCH my sister is. And if she doesn't apologize to me RIGHT NOW for leaving me, I am going to pour this glass of water onto her head!" she exclaimed. Time slowed down. I surveyed the faces at the table, which—shockingly—appeared sympathetic to my sister. I saw the people in the restaurant staring. No one interceded on my behalf. No one told her to sit down and behave. During that split second, I weighed my options. There was no way in hell that I was going to apologize to my sister. I hadn't done anything wrong. I also knew that if I didn't apologize, she really would pour the glass of water onto my head, and with pleasure. I wasn't going to give her that pleasure, so I pushed my chair back, and to the astonishment of everyone, walked out of the restaurant.

The surprises for the day weren't over yet. When I arrived at home, my sister had trashed my apartment. She took all of the clothes in my closet and threw them on the floor. All of the picture frames on my chest of drawers were on the floor and there were deep gashes in the top. I sat in my pile of clothes and sobbed. She had destroyed my apartment and turned my entire family against me. She used her time at the restaurant alone to indoctrinate my family and tell them her story about what a bitch I was. After the brunch, one by one they called and scolded me, unwilling or unable to see and hear my side of the story—even after I shared with them that she had trashed my apartment. I felt like I was living in opposite world. How was it that her behavior was okay? Why did my family see me through this lens?

My role in my family was to exist by living in the shadows: my sister's shadow, my father's shadow, my grandmother's shadow, shadows to avoid conflict or hide out. Each time I moved out of the shadows and stood in the light, I was shamed or blamed back into the shadows. Shadows were safe. But one can't thrive in the shadows. I had merely existed, receiving the bare minimum to survive. My entire life had been spent navigating the expectations of others to avoid notice. In my family, getting attention—at least for me—meant getting hurt.

While I was married to Jason, who is very private and unassuming, I conformed to his way of living. I continued the pattern of navigating the expectations of others to avoid notice. I was a member of the Junior League of Austin. I sat on a number of boards. We were members of Barton Creek Country Club. We attended all the right galas. Our kids went to the "right" schools and camps. We had a group of couples that all did things together. Our kids played together. In short, I "fit in." Yet, I was miserable. In order to fit in, I had to conform my life to meet the expectations of others. I wasn't able to express myself freely. I was suffocating. To breathe and survive, I blew it all up by getting divorced. Suddenly, my marriage, my life, and my choices had a spotlight shining on them. I could no longer hide in the shadows. My life was instantly under a microscope. For the first time in my life, I was forced to step out in full view. I was a life force on my own. People could no longer diminish me by attributing my accomplishments to a man.

In 2010, after divorcing Jason, I bought a home in the tony area of Pemberton Heights in Austin. When we divorced, Jason suggested that I consider renting. "You'll never be able to buy a home without me," he said. The country was in the midst of the mortgage and financial meltdown. People were over-leveraged and losing their homes right and left. I was lucky enough to find new construction in a fantastic central neighborhood and a builder motivated to sell. I had landed a beautiful new home in a great neighborhood with excellent schools. This was a great way to start off my new life.

To celebrate, I decided to throw a housewarming party. I hired a caterer, a DJ, and a photographer. We strung lights from the house to the garage and across the backyard. We set up a bar in the garage and had a signature cocktail. Cocktail tables with orchids were scattered across the yard, and waiters passed hors d'oeuvres. I hired an interior designer to decorate my home and it was filled with stylish furniture, art, and accessories. This was the first time that I had bought a house all by myself and the way that it was decorated was a reflection of me. The photographer wandered the party and took candids. The turnout was fantastic. Everyone kept telling me how beautiful the house looked and that I looked great.

A few days later, the photographer sent me the photos, which I posted to Facebook. Selecting my favorite one of me, I changed my profile picture. This was the new Carrie. Unencumbered by having to please anyone else, I was being my true self. I finally was stepping out of the shadows and letting my light shine. I was excited for what the world had in store for me.

I was very busy with work and travel whenever I didn't have my boys, so I missed a dinner at Uchiko, a popular sushi restaurant, with some of my closest friends. These were the girls that had been my ride-or-die for the past decade. We had all bonded through a book group that I had founded a decade earlier, which we called the Chick-lits. We had been there for each other through conception questions to pregnancies, breastfeeding issues, choosing doctors and babysitters, and the like. Many of our husbands were friends. So, I was sad to miss this dinner and called my friend Chloe, who had participated, as soon as I returned to hear how it went. Chloe asked me to come by her house for a glass of wine to catch up.

I was excited to see my friend. She poured us each a glass of wine. Then she said, "I wanted you to come over because we, the girls, are really concerned about you." I looked at her puzzled. "What? I'm doing great!" I was still reveling in the success of my housewarming party. She shook her head in disagreement and motioned for me to come sit at the kitchen counter. "It's your profile picture on Facebook," she said. "The girls are referring to it as the 'boob picture.'"

In the process of the divorce, I lost thirty pounds. I'd had a "mommy makeover." Now with a flat stomach and my boobs back where they belonged, I was looking and feeling great. When I was nursing, my breasts were enormous. My nursing bra was a 34F. With my petite frame, during those nursing years, I resembled a small gorilla. I nursed both boys for a year each, so when I was done, I was left with two enormous "rocks in a sock." I joked, "When you start to resemble the centerfold for *National Geographic* more than the centerfold for *Playboy*, it's time for plastic surgery!" The pregnancies and the nursing left me with a lot of breast tissue. The doctor told me that he could do a lift, but to fill out the top half of my bra, a small implant would help. I agreed and he did a breast lift and inserted small implants—250 cc each. I was ecstatic with the results. I referred to my new breasts as "mostly me." I was now a 34D and my boobs looked amazing.

Chloe opened up her laptop on the kitchen counter and pulled up Facebook. She navigated to my page and enlarged my profile picture. In this picture, I was wearing the dress I wore at the party —a fitted V-neck dress with ruching down the sides—giving the effect of being fitted but not too tight. The V-neck ended midchest so that there was zero cleavage exposed. I was turned slightly to the side, so the picture captured my curves. "I don't understand. What's wrong with this picture?" I asked. "Well, all we see in the picture is boobs. It's like you are displaying your sexuality." I felt myself become beet red. It felt like steam was coming out of my ears. I was awash in shame and anger. "There is nothing wrong with this picture. That's me at the party. Everyone was telling me how beautiful I looked. There is no cleavage. Nothing."

Chloe was unmovable. This message wasn't coming just from her. It was coming from every one of the group of friends who attended that dinner. I felt anger build as I thought about *my friends*, the book group that I founded and nurtured for a decade, talking about me. They had all attended the housewarming party. Turning again to the picture, she said, "What do you think your boys would think? You don't want your boys to be embarrassed of their mom, do you?" Shame. She was trying to shame me by using my children. I felt the room begin to spin. My light was going out, the world was getting dark. She continued, pushing the laptop toward me, "Let's change your profile picture right now. Let me help you select another one." She literally made me change my profile picture right then and there. I was numb and desperate to leave, so I acquiesced.

The famous "boob photo" that almost ended my life.

When I returned home, I sat in my bedroom and sobbed. I had shown the world my authentic self and it had been rejected. My light so bright that my "friends" rushed to put it out.

A week later, Chloe was being featured on the cover of a local magazine and there was a reception in her honor. I had been traveling, so I made sure that my flight arrived back in time to attend the reception. I rushed home to change out of my suit and threw on one of Diane von Furstenberg's iconic wrap dresses. I arrived just on time. Chloe worked the room and when she arrived at me, instead of thanking me for showing up for her, she reached across and adjusted my wrap dress to conceal more of my cleavage. Then, with a frown, a look of concern, and a shake of the head, she moved on. Stunned, I ran out of the room, tears flowing down my face, humiliated.

I began to feel myself sink into a depression. I would wake up in the middle of the night with tears flowing down my face. I was broken. A few days later, I was supposed to fly to Atlanta, and I couldn't get out of bed. I wanted to kill myself. I was having serious thoughts about suicide. I couldn't stop crying. Then, I remembered the wisdom I had learned from therapy: depression is anger turned inward. I was angry!! I wasn't just angry; I was fucking pissed! How dare my so-called friends treat me this way? Weren't they supposed to stand by me, stand up for me, cheer me on? I picked up the phone and called Chloe. "I have been lying here in bed, thinking about killing myself because of this BULLSHIT over my profile picture. In one fell swoop, you shamed me, brought my kids into it, and removed my support network! I am fucking PISSED! HOW DARE YOU! I'm pissed at you, and Birdie, and all the other girls who were at that dinner. You weren't *concerned* for me, you were *threatened* by me, and how dare you gang up on me! When they started talking about me at dinner, why didn't you stand up for me? You know me better than that! This is utter BULLSHIT!" I began to fill with rage and this rage propelled me out of bed and into action. I went to my computer and changed my profile picture back to the "boob picture." FUCK THEM.

Later that day, flowers and notes of apology appeared on my doorstep, but the damage had been done. Our relationships would never be the same. I dissolved the book group and sought out new friends. This wasn't easy. We had schools, friends, and activities in common. I tried to reorient myself to my new world—being the only single mom in my group of friends—but it was a constant struggle.

I came to realize that many of my married friends envied me. I had a career, so I could walk away from an unhappy marriage and maintain my standard of living. They were trapped in marriages with no way out—so much easier to throw darts at me than to examine their own lives. They were also trapped because they were constantly trying to "fit in" and "keep up with the Joneses." I was free from that in theory, but they were constantly trying to put me back into the box.

Four or five years later, one of the girls who attended the infamous "boob photo" dinner at Uchiko, Birdie (who had since been divorced herself), invited me to come over to her house to celebrate New Year's Eve. Another member of our former book group, Amelia, was also going through a divorce. It would just be the three of us having a quiet New Year's Eve together—well, us and Birdie's house painter (who was staying with her), but she promised he would stay out of the way.

Birdie and I shared a love for Sonoma-Cutrer Chardonnay, so I brought a bottle with me, and she had two bottles chilling already. Amelia brought her own bottle. Birdie had already been drinking, and there were a few friends there who had stopped by for wine and cheese before heading to their parties. The evening started out with Amelia filling us in on the details of what led to her divorce. Her divorce lawyer was a close friend of mine, so I was keen to hear about the advice she had been giving. As Amelia told her story, Birdie kept interrupting and inserting negative inferences and barbs. I found myself becoming defensive for Amelia, countering with words of comfort and empathy.

As I went to get my second glass of wine, I noticed that of three bottles of Sonoma-Cutrer, there was only half a bottle left. The conversation turned to dating after divorce. As I began to share my thoughts, Birdie interrupted. "Don't listen to her. Don't

take her advice. You should HEAR what people say about Carrie!"
she slurred. My jaw dropped as she rambled on: "Annie says they all
make fun of the tight pants you wear to the school in the morning!"
I replied, "You mean the James Perse leggings I wear?" I lived in
a great neighborhood, and the women who showed up at school
wore an assortment of Lululemon, tennis skirts, and yoga pants.
This was a good-looking crowd: sucked and tucked and botoxed. As
a single mom, I would roll out of bed and grab a pair of oversized
James Perse leggings and a T-shirt. I would be lucky to brush my
hair and teeth. It was not uncommon for me to appear with tooth-
paste on my face or a stain on my shirt. I didn't have time to get to
the gym. It was all work and all kids all the time. I was lucky that
I could afford a nanny. She was my saving grace. I only appeared
glamorous on my weekends off and when I had to attend a business
meeting. This girl was spreading vicious gossip. She had no idea
what she was talking about.

In the years since the boob picture, I learned to take things less
personally. I really didn't care what they were saying about me. I
knew my truth. I laughed off Birdie's comments and tried to change
the subject. But she wasn't done. Not by a long shot.

"You know what else they say about you?" she asked, refilling
her glass with wine. As best I could calculate, she was two bottles
in and there was no stopping her. She continued, "They say you
are always hitting on the men on your street. You invite them in
and try to seduce them!" This was truly laughable. There wasn't a
man on my street who was worthy of a second glance, let alone a
seduction attempt!! "Tell me more!" I said. As the story unfolded,
what I learned was that at some point, years earlier, I had offered
a neighbor a beer—a moment so insignificant to me that I couldn't

recall it. This act of neighborhood friendliness had been magnified into me being a slut, a husband-stealing seductress. I was actually laughing at this point because it was so totally absurd.

But Birdie wasn't done: "You think this is FUNNY? Didn't you ever wonder why your boys stopped getting invited to birthday parties?"

She had gone too far. My boys *had* stopped being invited to birthday parties. I had noticed and it crushed me. My heart broke for my boys. These nasty rumors had directly and permanently impacted my boys' lives. None of it was true. It was all lies. The cost was so high.

I sold my house in Pemberton Heights and my boys changed schools, but it didn't get easier. The truth is that celebrating your uniqueness isn't easy. People like things that line up, fit, are the same. Moreover, my *role* in my friends' lives had changed—I had always been the one providing help in the background. Like a background singer now taking a lead role, I was standing on my own and getting attention, which took attention away from them. I made a more concerted effort to surround myself with friends whom I call my "circle of light." These are friends who celebrate my successes, lift me up, provide support, and challenge me in constructive ways. These are the friends who pushed me to write this book.

CHAPTER TEN

PROPHET OR SPIRITUAL ASSASSIN?

*"I distrust those people who know so well what
God wants them to do, because I notice it
always coincides with their own desires."*

—SUSAN B. ANTHONY

As I reached adulthood, my father's narcissism only became
more pronounced. My therapist described him as a malignant
narcissist. The worst kind on the spectrum of narcissism. A
malignant narcissist is characterized by an inability to appreciate
others, a sense of entitlement, lack of authenticity, need for control, delusional thinking, intolerance of the views/opinions of
others, emotional detachment, grandiosity, lack of awareness or
concern regarding the impact of their behavior, minimal emotional

reciprocity, and a desperate need for the approval and positive attention of others.

When I was married to Beaux, my father sent a letter to his children. I refer to the letter as the "Demand Letter." In this letter he started out by quoting scripture (Exodus 21:12): "Honor your father and your mother, so that you may live long in the land the Lord your God is giving you." My father noted that of the Ten Commandments, this is the only one that comes with a promise—the promise of long life. He wrote that the opposite was also true: if we did not honor him, our lives would be cut short. With his twist on this scripture, he provided a list of demands. He wanted each of his three children to invite him for Thanksgiving and Christmas and other events. He also had a list of expectations for how we were supposed to behave and interact with him. He went on to describe how if we did not meet his list of demands we would be cursed. This letter sent chills through me. It was pure evil. I ripped the letter up and then burned it. I called my brother and sister and warned them, "Don't open it. It's evil. Burn it." His words fucked with my head.

After sending the letter, my parents traveled to Austin to visit Beaux and me for Christmas. I dreaded seeing them. They rented a time-share on Lake Travis since we did not have room for them. We visited them on Christmas Day and my father engaged in his usual antics—he would ask probing and inappropriate questions and then pass judgment and lecture me about my answers. He didn't respect boundaries, always leaving me extremely uncomfortable. It was an unusually hot Christmas that year, with temperatures in the eighties. My father reached into his suitcase to hand me my Christmas gift. It was an unwrapped oversized angora sweater with a huge teddy bear on it. "I picked this up at Costco for you," my father said, shoving the sweater at me. It was too much for me to handle graciously. Memories of past gifts came rushing back. My thirteenth birthday—a down sleeping bag from REI—just what every teen girl wants! I felt like I was suffocating. "Wow, what a perfect gift for Texas weather! I can just see myself wearing this in court!" I said. My father, to the extent that he saw me, saw me as a little girl. He never gave me what I wanted. He didn't even care to ask or wonder what I might like. His thoughtlessness paired with his demands was just too much.

Sometime after my parents returned to Seattle, my father called me in a panic. He told me that he had been hired to give expert testimony in a court case in Portland. He had given the plaintiff's attorney his expert opinion and written up a report. Based on his opinion, the plaintiff's attorney decided not to settle, but to take the case to trial. On the drive from Seattle to Portland, my father was thinking over his testimony and "felt God telling him" that he should change it. My father told me that at trial he offered an opinion that was exactly the opposite of what he had put in his report and that the plaintiff's attorney had relied upon. My father was upset because the plaintiff's attorney became unhinged and started screaming at my father. It was only then that my father snapped out of his delusional thinking and grandiosity and real- ized that his change of opinion impacted others—negatively. He was calling me because he was worried that he might get sued. "I don't think an expert can get sued for changing his opinion unless it can be proven that he was somehow compromised," I told my father. "But your bigger concern here is that you are going to get blacklisted. I doubt many lawyers are going to want to hire you after that stunt."

But my father's delusional thinking and grandiosity consumed him. When I visited him shortly after my divorce from Jason, he took me to dinner. It was one of the longest dinners of my life. For more than three hours, I was trapped and forced to listen to my father's rantings. At this dinner, he proclaimed to me that he was a prophet, like the great prophets in the Bible. When I looked at him in disbelief, he told me that when I got to heaven, God would tell me that my father was a prophet. He talked about how sick society is, and how crooked the Church is. "God is an angry God!" he proclaimed. "God's wrath is imminent! Just you wait!"

Having been kicked out of countless churches, my father started his own "home church." He wrote two books criticizing the Christian church and the "lukewarm Christian." His books contained his "prophecies" about the Church, lukewarm Christians, and the wrath of God. My father acted as judge and jury. He knew who was a "true Christian." Somehow, in his twisted thinking, my father had forgotten that "Christian" meant a follower of Christ, and Christ died on the cross to *forgive* the sins of his followers. God's wrath was surpassed by the grace of God and his forgiveness. My father had conveniently skipped past God's command in Matthew 7:1 that we "Judge not, lest ye be judged." According to Mark 12:31, God's greatest commandment is to "love thy neighbor," not judge thy neighbor! But somehow this was lost on my father. Judging others made him feel powerful and superior and fed his narcissism. I escaped that dinner, but I will never forget it.

My father came to visit me and the boys in Austin for Christmas in 2011. My mother had been in assisted living for four years at this point. My father was the one "living" grandparent left. Both of my grandfathers passed before I was born, and I really missed having that loving grandparent experience—I wanted it so much for my boys. So, I tried to encourage positive interactions with my father, but when you are dealing with a malignant narcissist, that can be impossible.

My father insisted that I wait on him hand and foot as my mother did. He would plunk himself down on the couch and ask that I bring him a drink or make him some lunch. He would pick up a book and start reading and ignore the kids, who were anxious to get attention from their granddad. He inquired about how much money I made, how much my house was worth, what accolades the boys or I had received. Narcissists see their kids as extensions of themselves and he loved to co-opt my achievements as his own. He would ask inappropriate questions and then pass judgment on my answers. He didn't respect boundaries. In short, he was exhausting and emotionally draining to deal with.

My father was reading, and the boys were playing with their toys, so I took the opportunity to run upstairs and take a shower. It wasn't long before I heard screams, then sobs, and footsteps running up the stairs, followed by more sobbing. I thought the boys had gotten in a fight. I rushed toward the boys' bedrooms to see who had come flying up the stairs. I found Tommy in his bunk bed, wracked with sobs, the covers pulled over his head. I climbed up to him and, easing the covers down, I pulled him close to me. "Honey, what happened?" I asked, as I brushed his hair to the side and kissed his cheek. "Did your brother hit you?" "NO! GRANDPA did!" he sobbed. My world started to spin; my stomach sank. I was filled with rage. "Tommy, tell me EXACTLY what happened," I asked as calmly as I could. "GRANDPA CHOKED ME!" he sobbed as his body shook. He was in so much pain.

I ran down the stairs and confronted my father. "What the holy fuck happened? What did you do to my son?" I asked tersely, hands on hips. My father was once again sitting reading. He looked at me completely nonplussed, and replied, "The boys were roughhousing. They were out of control. You need to discipline them more." I looked at Andy. "What did he do?" Andy was hiding under a desk. I pulled him out and wrapped my arms around him. "Tell me what happened," I asked as I held him tight. "Grandpa threw Tommy against the wall and choked him," Andy matter-of-factly replied. My father continued to read. "Did you choke Tommy?" I asked him. "They were out of control. He needed to be disciplined." No apology. No regret. Just justification. I felt anger flush through my body. My maternal grandmother had been allowed to decimate me emotionally. No one had ever interceded on my behalf. I was forced to interact with her and be subject to her lethal barbs. My father had hurt me, but he would not be allowed to hurt my boys. I would never do to my boys what my parents had done to me. I felt resolve pulse through me. It was Christmas Day. "You will leave in the morning. You will never be allowed to see your grandkids again. DO YOU UNDERSTAND ME?" I went back upstairs to comfort Tommy. "Honey, you never have to see him again. Ever. I will protect you. I am so, so sorry that he hurt you." My heart broke for my kids. I wanted so badly for them to experience the love of grandparents. Instead, they had experienced the toxicity and abuse that was my father. But no more. I would love them fiercely and give them the emotional resources they needed to set boundaries. The family chain of malignant narcissism ended that night. It was a painful end, but also a bright new beginning—a Christmas gift.

CHAPTER ELEVEN

DEMENTIA & DEATH

"Carve your name on hearts, not tombstones.
A legacy is etched into the minds of others and
the stories that they share about you."

—SHANNON ALDER

After we returned from Jason's mother, Elizabeth's, funeral, my father reached out asking to come visit us in Austin. I had been counting on Elizabeth to help with the baby. After her sudden death, I was devastated to lose her, but also had to support my newborn son and my husband, who had lost both parents in the period of a year. I was hopeful that my mother could be a support and teach me a few things, so we agreed to let them come for a visit.

After they arrived, my mother asked if she could go for a swim in our pool, and my father pulled me aside to talk to me. I watched my mother as she struggled to figure out how to get into the pool. She started to try to go into the deep end. I opened our French doors and showed her where the steps into the pool were located. Back inside, my father spoke: "I had your mother tested. She either has Alzheimer's or frontal lobe dementia." As my father explained, I watched my mother emerge from the pool and begin to strip naked. I left him midsentence, opening the French doors again and running outside to stop her from completely removing her swimsuit. It was obvious she was really struggling.

I went back inside and lifted my precious, newborn baby and cradled him to my chest. I was overwhelmed by a sense of loss. My beautiful baby had lost both of his paternal grandparents, and now my mom. My mom wasn't available to offer me support. I felt incredibly alone. I was also terrified. Would I get dementia? Was this what life had in store for me?

With my mother at our home in Everett before her light began to dim.

As per usual, my father was completely insensitive to his timing. Why did he have to tell me this now, within weeks of Elizabeth's death? It felt so cruel, like pouring acid on an open wound.

My heart broke for my mother. She had endured so much with my father. It just seemed wrong for her to get robbed again.

My mother was put on medications that seemed to slow her decline. My father, on the other hand, proceeded full steam ahead on the train to share his prophecies. He took her on mission trips to China and to Africa, which terrified me because he never paid her much attention.

In 2007, my sister married Allan Hunter. About an hour before the wedding, my father dropped my mother off at my hotel room so that I could help her get dressed. He handed me her dress and shoes and told me that he would see me at the wedding. My best friend from high school, Stephanie Engnes, was accompanying me to the wedding and we were sharing a hotel room. We were rushing to get ready and now had my mom to contend with. As we helped her to get undressed, we saw that her legs were unshaved, and her armpit hair was inches long. Stephanie and I began to panic. My mom looked like a homeless person. What was going on? Wasn't my father taking care of my mother? What were we going to do? There wasn't time to completely shave her.

Stephanie and I found a pair of pantyhose that camouflaged the leg hair and found a small bolero jacket to cover her armpit hair. We stepped back to look at the result and realized that she had food stuck in her teeth. As Stephanie and I worked to brush and floss her teeth, we were disgusted by the condition of her teeth. There was food caught everywhere and her teeth were black. It was clear that my father was not brushing her teeth.

I was not dressed yet so Stephanie took my mother to the wedding, and I rushed to pull myself together. I arrived after the wedding had started. I walked in just as my name was called to do a reading of scripture.

My mom looked good. Stephanie and I had done a miraculous job of pulling her together. I was pissed at my father and made a beeline for him at the reception. "Listen, it is clear that Mom isn't getting properly bathed or cared for. Her teeth were disgusting. When is the last time her teeth were brushed?" My father responded, "I put her in the shower and tell her to wash her hair and shave her legs and she just stands there. I remind her to brush her teeth, but I guess she doesn't do it?" I could not believe what I was hearing. "If you tell a baby to change its diaper, do you expect that to happen, too?" I retorted. I knew that my father didn't "see" her, that he viewed her as an extension of himself, but I was shocked that he could lie in bed at night with a woman who didn't bathe, shave her legs or armpits, or brush her teeth and not notice her condition—at least the *smell* of her. I treated my dog better.

At my insistence, my father hired a woman to help bathe and feed my mother. Shortly thereafter, I received a call from one of my siblings that my mother was being moved into an assisted living facility—she had defecated in their bed—something my father couldn't ignore.

The following Mother's Day, I went with my girlfriends, Shannon and Ashley, to The Phoenecian in Scottsdale for a spa weekend. My parents were living in nearby Carefree, so my father offered to pick me up and take me to go see my mother. We stopped for lunch on the way. At the restaurant, my father talked on and on about this woman, Susan, whom he had been spending time with. I was beginning to fume. My mother had devoted her life to this man. She had given up everything for him—her friends, her family, her very identity—and she is in assisted living for less than a year and he had already taken up with another woman? What had happened to his Christian beliefs? Suddenly, they weren't convenient anymore? I interrupted him: "So what's the deal with this Susan woman? Are you having an affair?" He stammered around, finally answering, "It's just lust." I told him how incredibly disrespectful I found his behavior to be. "I cannot believe that you are sitting here telling your daughter about another woman on Mother's Day," I said shaking my head in disgust.

We went to see my mother and he would not let me be alone with her. What was he afraid of? Did he think that I would tell her? She didn't recognize me. She just sat there and smiled and nodded with a blank look on her face. I was crushed.

I took my boys to see her a couple of times after that. I asked my youngest, Andy, if he understood what was wrong with Grandma. Just four at the time, he replied perfectly, "Yeah, Grandma got her brain jacked!" He would never know the love or affection of a grandparent. My heart broke for him.

In the early morning hours after Christmas of 2012, my mother passed away, nine painful years after her diagnosis. I could finally grieve her loss.

I looked back on her bizarre behavior leading up to her diagnosis and wondered how much of it was the disease, how much of it was her? I blamed my father for the early onset of her disease. My mother had stopped thinking for herself decades earlier. She had given herself up so completely to my father that he controlled every aspect of her life. She had no meaningful friendships. No social outlets other than church and bible studies. She didn't watch television, read, work, exercise, or do anything to stretch or energize her brain or body. I had a profound sense of loss—not just because of her death, but because I never really had much of a mom. She was so focused on my father that she took little interest in us. She had no interest in the things moms usually joyfully help their daughters with—picking out a prom dress or planning a wedding. She wasn't available to help with makeup, hair, fashion, or dating. My sister and I raised ourselves (which explains some really bad hair, makeup, and fashion choices!). As I reflected back on all of this, I found deep compassion and forgiveness for my mother. She didn't have the support or resources she needed to show up as a mom. She was doing the best that she could. I also found immense gratitude for having a sister. As tortured as our relationship had been growing up, we understood each other and began to lean on one another for unconditional love, encouragement, support, and nonjudgment.

I flew to Seattle for my mother's funeral. As per usual, my best friend from high school, Stephanie Engnes, showed up for me. She picked me up from the airport and let me stay at her house. She went to the funeral with me. At the funeral, my father pranced around like he was the belle of the ball. Like always, this was his moment and all about him. As people stood up and spoke about my mother, they told stories about what a great Christian example she was and how she had counseled them on being submissive to their husbands. I looked around the room and wanted to scream at them, *Whatever she told you, it was all lies!* She was miserable! She was chronically depressed. Her commitment to being submissive is what killed her! My brother stood up and spoke: "My mother was a terrible cook..." My sister and I burst out laughing. It was true!

She was a terrible cook! But when you are that controlled, you tend to lose your creativity. She had waited on my father hand and foot, making every one of his meals—she did the bare minimum—but there was no joy in it. A good friend of my father's stood up to defend her. After first shaming my brother for speaking the truth, she said, "Your mother was NOT a terrible cook! I remember a time I went over to her house for lunch and she made me a frozen pizza!" Ha! My brother and sister and I burst into laughter again. The whole scene was totally surreal. We felt like we were in an alternate reality. The woman that these religious zealots spoke of was not the mother that we knew. I walked out of the funeral and into the church parking lot and screamed loud and long into the night air. Then, turning to Stephanie, I commanded, "I need to get drunk. *Really* drunk. Take me to a bar." She took me to Arnie's in Mukilteo for some shots, then stayed up with me late into the night as I sobbed and shook with grief. I was so grateful to have a friend who knew my family and truly understood what I was going through. She showed up for me, offered me comfort and solace, let me grieve without judgment, and stood steadfastly by my side.

I was the first of my friends to lose a parent. And my mom had been sick for nine years. I told a few close friends that my mom had passed and each of them said, "She's been sick for a really long time, right? It must be a relief." I wanted to scream at them in agony, "NO, it's not a relief! I miss my mom! I miss the mom I wish I had! I feel cheated! I'm fucking pissed! My mom's life was a waste! She never really LIVED!" I didn't receive a single card or flowers; the only support I got was from Stephanie. It was more like my friends were relieved to not have to hear about my mom anymore. I felt so incredibly alone.

I reached out to my best friend from college, Stephanie Wood-ard, to tell her the news. I didn't get the chance. When I spoke to her, she told me that her colon cancer was back and that it had metastasized to her brain. This was like a body blow to me. Didn't God know that it was unfair to kick someone when they were down? Stephanie passed away seven months after my mother. I yelled at God. Stephanie was a life force. She lived and loved passionately. Smart, creative, and hysterically funny, she was and is an inspiration to me. I felt robbed.

As I struggled with depression from so much loss, I heard Stephanie Woodard's voice: "Oh my God, get it together! You are still THERE! You still have a LIFE to LIVE!!! Take life by the balls!!"

As I grieved their losses, I started to wonder how I might live my life differently. What lessons had I learned from their lives? I reflected on other friends and family whom I had lost. My friend Cindy Bourland had lost her husband some years earlier. At his funeral, I learned that he carried around a personal mission state-ment in his wallet—and he really lived by it.[2] In his short life, he lived life to the fullest and left an impact on everyone he met. He was genuine and selfless. When my friend David Walter passed away, he filled 3,000 seats at his funeral. One after another, people spoke and said, "He was my best friend..." David lived in Blue Lake, Texas, and drove the hour and a half into Austin every day for work. Each morning, he would stop at the same gas station to buy coffee. The gas station attendant who sold him that coffee each morning visited him in the hospital and spoke at his funeral! David took the time every day to stop and ask the gas station attendant about

---

2   The text of his personal mission statement is included in the Appendix.

his life and family. Mike Bourland did the same thing. These were people whom I wanted to emulate.

I thought about Stephanie Woodard. She was so engaged in life. She had thousands of friends. She had an immense impact on so many lives. I thought of my father's mother, Bahma. A true original, she was always her authentic self. She was fun, funny, and magnetic. When she would enter a room filled with young people, they would all flock to her. She made an impression and touched people's hearts. I thought of my mother and what her life could have been. I thought of the choices she made and the high cost of them. There were gifts in all of this loss. I realized who I didn't want to be and who I did. I learned the importance of the choices that we make. I thought about what I wanted on my tombstone, whom I wanted at my funeral. I decided that I would live each day as if it were my last. I vowed to express my gratitude in the moment. I tell people that I love, admire, respect, and appreciate them—in the moment. I pay attention to my interactions with others—I try to always be gracious and kind—because I don't know if that interaction may be my or their last on this planet. I say yes to more opportunities because they may never come again. I try to make the most of every moment and to be present in it.

As I reflected on this, I embraced the teachings of Deepak Chopra in his book *The Seven Spiritual Laws of Success*: "Anytime that I come into contact with someone, I will give them something —a smile, a prayer, a compliment, my attention, a blessing, an act of service, caring, attention, affection, or appreciation." I choose actions that bring happiness and success to others. This is my daily practice. This is my legacy.

CHAPTER TWELVE

LOSING MY BEST FRIEND TO CANCER

"To live in hearts we leave behind is not to die."

—THOMAS CAMPBELL

We met at the University of Texas at Austin Alumni Center. We were both there to attend a meeting of the Student Involvement Committee, known as SIC. Stephanie Dugger Woodard was an Alpha Chi Omega and I had affiliated with the Tri Delt house at Texas. I was new to the university and anxious to make new friends. She made it easy. She was so damn funny. Quick-witted and sarcastic, I could always count on Stephanie for a funny story or wicked quip. She had beautiful, thick, long brown hair, big brown eyes, great legs, and a sassy attitude that men loved. She was energetic and magnetic, and people flocked to her.

We would drink margaritas at Baby Acapulco's or play spades, drink beers, eat peanuts, and smoke cloves at Cain & Abel's. Once when I took a drag off a cigarette, I joked, "My father is lucky he is a lung doctor; can you imagine what I would be like if he was a gynecologist?" She laughed. "Speaking of gynecologists, my boyfriend Len and I were having sex the other night and the contraceptive sponge I used got stuck!! I couldn't get it out! Len was great. He turned his baseball cap around, threw my legs in the air and said, 'I'm going in!' He was in up to his wrist! But he got it out!" I couldn't stop laughing at this visual.

Stephanie grew up in Round Rock, Texas, which is just north of Austin, where her father was an attorney. She talked about her father a lot. How much she admired him and wanted to be like him. I was envious of their relationship.

After college, we lost touch. But then one day, I ran into her at the annual Whitehurst Harkness Christmas party, a party encompassing three floors of a capital area office building, which hundreds of lawyers attended. We were both lawyers now. She was practicing family law. We were overjoyed to see one another and promised that we would never lose touch again.

We met for lunch later that week and she filled me in on what had transpired in the years that I had missed. One day, out of nowhere, her father abandoned his legal practice and his family and moved to Colorado, never to be heard from again. The State Bar of Texas had to come in and transfer his client files to other attorneys and shut down his practice. He was disbarred for abandoning his clients. Stephanie was heartbroken and devastated. Her boyfriend, Len, whom I remembered from college, stepped up and paid for her health insurance while she continued law school.

She and Len later married. I was stunned by her news and sad that I hadn't been there to support her through her devastating loss.

Stephanie had been the Social Chair for the Austin Young Lawyers Committee and encouraged me to take the job after her. I did this gladly. With her, there was always a fun party to plan or to attend. She was a natural hostess and an outstanding cook. We were there for each other through pregnancies and childbirths. She handled both of my divorces. As a divorce attorney, she was practical and unemotional. She gave sage advice.

Eventually, she and Len moved to Fort Worth, Texas. I was extremely sad when they moved away. It was as if part of my heart had left. But it was a good move for them, and they ended up loving Fort Worth.

I had my fortieth birthday party upstairs in a private room at the Starlite Café in downtown Austin. It was an intimate affair. I invited ten of my closest friends. I brought gifts for each of them and a handwritten note for each explaining how much I valued them and the role that they had played in my life. I was embracing the ethos "live each day as if it is your last." It made sense to me to express how I felt now because at forty, who knew how much time we had left?

As we were leaving the party, Stephanie pulled me aside. "I'm really scared," she said. "I've been bleeding a lot from my asshole. Like I'm having a freakin' period, but from the wrong hole! I have an appointment with a doctor on Monday to find out what's going on." Her words terrified me. What the hell was going on?

She called me a few days later. "It's cancer," she said, "I'm going in for emergency surgery tomorrow. I'll know more then." The diagnosis came back: stage III colon cancer. They removed a tumor which had penetrated the wall of her colon and the cancer was in one lymph node. She sounded frightened.

My husband, Jason, commissioned a painting for me for my fortieth birthday. The artist, Kathy Womack, working from photos, painted a picture of me with three of my closest friends around a birthday cake. Stephanie was one of the friends whom she had painted. As I thought about Stephanie, I traced the painting of her, grateful that I had it.

As per usual, Stephanie approached cancer as she did everything: with wit and humor. We joked about how she was kicking cancer in the ass. She did her chemotherapy and lost her hair but never her humor. The news came back that she was in remission. We breathed a collective sigh of relief.

To celebrate her remission, we planned a trip to Cabo San Lucas. I was newly divorced for the second time and looking forward to relaxing on the beach. Stephanie had another mission. When she had been in Cabo San Lucas some years before, she met a woman named Patricia who sold necklaces in a downtown market. Stephanie spent some time talking with her and purchased an assortment of necklaces from her. The necklaces were such a hit in Texas that Stephanie was determined to help this woman sell them to her friends. I committed to helping Stephanie find Patricia.

It didn't take us long to locate her. She was working in the same booth in the market. As we talked to her, we learned that while she was extremely poor, she volunteered at the local shelter for battered women. We were in awe. We wanted to help, so we took her to Costco to buy underwear and supplies for the shelter. When we got into the car, I insisted that she sit in front, the place of honor. I understood now why Stephanie had been so touched by her and wanted to find her again. Stephanie paid for a deposit box at the post office so that they could stay in touch and Patricia agreed to send Stephanie necklaces to sell in the United States.

One of Stephanie's friends was a travel writer who had recently profiled a new resort in Cabo San Lucas called Capella Pedregal. A tunnel had been bored through a mountain so that guests could get to the resort from the town. Like something out of a James Bond movie, the tunnel had a series of huge chandeliers and opened to a breathtaking view of the beach. The resort itself was carved into the mountain. Each room was a villa with a plunge pool. Stephanie had been raving about it, so to surprise her, I changed our reservation and paid for two nights at this gorgeous resort. I was glad that I did; her friendship meant so much to me and this was a great way to end an epic trip.

Two years later, the colon cancer was back. It was in her liver. But she was also diagnosed with breast cancer. I traveled to Fort Worth to stay with her in the hospital during her liver surgery, hopeful that they would get all of the cancer. She did more chemo and seemed to improve, but I could tell she was really scared.

Then a year later, it had metastasized to her brain. I wanted to see her, but she kept putting me off. It wasn't a good time, she said. I felt an urgency to see her. I knew that there wasn't much time left. So, on the advice of a friend, I got in my car and drove from Austin to Fort Worth without an invitation. She was shocked and embarrassed to see me. "I wish you didn't see me like this!" she exclaimed. "My hair looks terrible, and my nails aren't done!" She had brain surgery with the Cyberknife and it left her confused and foggy. I didn't care. I didn't care how she looked or that she was struggling with her words. I just wanted her to know how much I loved her. I knew there wasn't much time—for the visit, because she tired quickly, or for her life. I got right to the point. "I'm here for you. And for your kids. I love you so much."

And then she was gone. Selfishly, I fucking missed her. She had been one of my pillars of support. On the heels of losing my mother, I felt totally lost.

Her funeral did not do her justice. Hundreds of people attended, but only her law school friends were invited to speak, so much of her greatness was left unspoken. Stephanie helped to get Debra Lehrman elected to the Texas Supreme Court, and she was there in attendance. The reception following was held in the church basement where store-bought cookies and coffee were offered. This was the moment I first heard her speak. Not literally, but a voice in my head. I could hear her saying, "I can't believe this wasn't catered. And there should be some beautiful flowers. And the church basement??" We had planned many parties together so I instinctively knew what she would have liked. The reception was not reflective of Stephanie. At. All. Stephanie had also written two novels. "What about that? How come no one mentioned that?" I heard her say.

And so it went. In my grief, I could hear her. "Look, I'm loving that you miss me so much. But, Jesus, you are still there! So, pull it together and go live!" Her voice is with me. She spurs me on to live the best, fullest life I can. To seize each moment. To take life by the balls. To love deeply and often. To cherish friendships. To lift others up. To have fun. And always to find the wit and humor in everything. She wasn't here long, but dammit, she left an impression on my soul.

CHAPTER THIRTEEN

RECOGNIZING EVIL

"Intuition is always right in at least two
important ways: it is always in response to something,
and it always has your best interest at heart."

—GAVIN DE BECKER

I saw my father one last time at my mother's funeral. He was
no longer permitted by me to have any contact with my boys, but I
had still been speaking to him because I had been concerned about
my mother's condition. At the funeral, he wore a black leather hat
and a long black leather coat. He looked like a Mafia henchman. His
signature scowl completed the look. After the burial, close family
members were invited to eat at Anthony's restaurant on the Everett
waterfront. I positioned myself as far away from him as I could, but
I could still overhear him talking loudly about how he was working
as the medical director of a biotech company. The company had

come up with a product that would revolutionize herpes treatment. Herpes was rampant in Africa, so they were going to begin to test their product there, and the company had a Christian mission component to it as well. He was going to make millions and convert thousands! Why would a biotech company focused on a herpes cure hire my father, a lung doctor? It made no sense.

My intuition started nagging at me. I recalled my father getting involved in an investment scheme with a "Christian" family when I was a child. The Larsens quickly became our best friends. Mrs. Larsen shared a brownie recipe with my mother that was one of our favorite treats. Apparently, the Larsens convinced my father to invest in a company that imported lumber from Japan. I was just a kid at the time, but I wondered why anyone would import lumber to the State of Washington, one of the timber capitals of the world. It was a con. The Larsens took our money. It wasn't until many years later that I realized my mother would whip up Mrs. Larsen's brownies whenever she was pissed at my father. She was passive-aggressive that way.

After the funeral, I called my father to get more details on his new gig. It took some probing, but he finally admitted that he was given the medical director role after he invested in the company. "How much money did you invest?" I asked. "$100,000," he replied. "How much money do the founders of the company have invested?" I asked. He hemmed and hawed and finally admitted that the founders didn't have any money in the company. Alarm bells were exploding in my head. "All of their money is tied up in their oil investments in Ukraine," he explained. I stopped him right there and asked him to give me the exact spelling of the involved people's names and to send me all the paperwork he had, including copies of any shares he had received. He located the paperwork, and it was only signed by him. He didn't have any stock certificates. This was bad. I got busy searching and recruited my sister to help. One of the founders of the company was a Canadian who was currently being extradited from England for tax fraud in Canada. The other couple involved had numerous lawsuits filed against them in Maricopa County—many by the same attorney. I called the attorney and told her what had happened to my father. She said that most of the victims were doctors and dentists, and that the money was likely already gone. I called my father back, told him what I had learned, and gave him the attorney's name. I called him a few weeks later and he told me that he had gotten his money back. I didn't believe him. There were so many lawsuits pending against this group of individuals—why would they give him his money back? I looked at his LinkedIn page. He had added "Director of Clinical Research" for the company. Of course, he could never be wrong. Even with all of the evidence we had provided him that he was dealing with crooks, he was still involved with the company. I was done. I realized in that moment that with my mother gone, I didn't need to speak with him anymore. I asked myself, *If every time you did something, it caused you severe pain and distress, would you continue to do it?* The answer was no. It became clear to me that it wasn't safe for me to continue to interact with him.

Over time, I came to forgive him for his abuse, neglect, grandiosity, and delusional thinking. The more I distanced myself, the more objectively I could view him. I came to pity him. There is power in pity. The people whom we pity have no control over us. We are released from their grip.

As I reflected on my decision, I read M. Scott Peck's *People of the Lie*. In his groundbreaking book, the author of *The Road Less Traveled* wrote, "The evil in this world is committed by the spiritual fat cats, by the Pharisees of our own day, the self-righteous who think they are without sin because they are unwilling to suffer the discomfort of significant self-examination." He continued,

> A predominant characteristic, however, of the behavior of those I call evil is scapegoating. Because in their hearts they consider themselves above reproach, they must lash out at anyone who does reproach them. They sacrifice others to preserve their self-image of perfection...Strangely enough, evil people are often destructive because they are attempting to destroy evil. The problem is that they misplace the locus of the evil. Instead of destroying others, they should be destroying the sickness within themselves. As life often threatens their self-image of perfection, they are often busily engaged in hating and destroying that life—usually in the name of righteousness.

I couldn't put the book down. He was talking about my father. Peck noted that evil people rarely reside in jail, their evil is so pervasive and subtle. They often manipulate others to achieve their evil goals.

Peck went on to describe how one could recognize evil. "The feeling that a healthy person often experiences in relationship with an evil one is revulsion. The feeling of revulsion may be almost instant if the evil encountered is blatant. If the evil is more subtle, the revulsion may develop only gradually as the relationship with the evil one slowly deepens." By the time that I was a teenager, I experienced revulsion whenever I was around my father. He made my skin crawl. I wanted to escape him. It became so bad that my parents acquiesced to me seeing a therapist—but it had to be a "Christian" one who agreed to report back to them everything that I said. I saw him once. I didn't trust him. I was terrified of what he would say to my parents.

Peck noted that another signal of evil is confusion. I experienced this with my father as well. He was so adept at twisting facts and scripture that I was often left confused. I didn't know what was true.

As I finished Peck's book, I realized that there was a gift in my experiences with my father—the gift of recognizing evil. When I was a child, our home became a regular place for bible studies, prayer groups, and other religious gatherings. My brother, sister, and I would hide out upstairs while these were going on and come down after they were over. One day, I came downstairs, and my parents were talking to this very tall, very large man with a dark beard and hair. He reminded me of Brutus from Popeye. He was introduced to me as "Bill." I took an immediate dislike to him. I stood there quietly listening to their conversation. After everyone was gone and the front door was locked, I told my parents, "Don't ever let that man into our house again. He's been to prison for rape, and he'll do it again." My parents stared at me dumbfounded and tried to dismiss me, but I begged them urgently to take me seriously. A few months later, Bill was kicked out of the church for attempting to rape someone. He had indeed been to prison for rape. Over my lifetime, there have been many other instances like this where I knew with absolute certainty that someone was dangerous and evil. What has been uncanny is how accurately I know what their *type* of evil is. For years I didn't understand how I knew, but I learned to trust my intuition. After reading *The Gift of Fear* and *People of the Lie*, I came to realize that my childhood had been a training ground for my intuition. My subconscious had learned how to recognize evil. This is truly a gift. What can be frustrating is that when I try to warn off a friend or colleague from someone whom I perceive to be trouble, they often don't perceive it and may dismiss my warning. As Peck noted, "Those who are evil are often charming and the pretense most commonly chosen by the evil is the pretense of love because it is designed to hide the opposite." It's very hard to see someone as evil when they are charming and *appear to be caring*.

The thing about intuition is that we often override it with our conscious mind. Our intuition tells us to be wary of someone, but then we talk ourselves out of it. We tell ourselves that we are being silly and dismiss the warning from our subconscious. I suspect that is what happened when I was raped. I was wary of following him upstairs but dismissed those thoughts as being silly—I was with several sorority sisters, after all. I didn't know that he had plans to separate me from them. Because of the rape, I now have a heightened sense of awareness. It's as if my intuition screams at me. My subconscious is less subtle, more aggressive about being heard. My conscious mind embraces the signals from the subconscious. I'm certainly not perfect, but I've come to see this heightened awareness as a gift.

CHAPTER FOURTEEN

WHEN LIFE GIVES YOU LEMONS

"Learn to laugh at yourself and you'll be entertained for life."

—UNKNOWN

If there is one lesson that life has taught me, it is that mindset is everything. When shit happens, choose happiness, humor, joy, and adventure, because life is one long roller coaster ride and you can scream the whole way or throw up your hands and enjoy the ride. We can't wait for the right partner, for hardship to end, or for life to be perfect before we are happy. Happiness is a choice, not a result or a destination. It is a mental decision. As Ralph Harston writes, "Nothing will make you happy until you choose to be happy. No person will make you happy until you decide to be happy. Your happiness will not come *to* you. It can only come *from* you." Thoughts precede actions. Our mindset—how we choose to think and view the world—predetermines outcomes. According to Roy T. Bennett, "Happiness is a choice. Optimism is a choice. Kindness is a choice. Giving is a choice. Respect is a choice. Whatever choice you make makes you. Choose wisely."

On one Vegas trip with my friend Sally we decided to stay at the Bellagio, a relatively new hotel at the time. Sally and I were excited to see the famous Bellagio fountains. To watch the fountains up close, we made a dinner reservation at Olives, which offered outdoor dining next to the fountains. Excited for a fun night out, Sally and I spent about two hours getting ready. All glammed up, we checked in at Olives and were seated on the outdoor balcony right next to the fountains. It was a windy night and just as we were paying our check, the wind caught the fountain just at the right moment, sending a tidal wave of water headed in our direction. Sally quickly ducked under an umbrella. I was not so lucky. Completely soaked with water from head to toe, I stood there shivering. Sally looked at me expectantly—would our night be ruined? Would I need to spend hours getting ready again? In that split second, standing there soaked, I knew that I had a choice to make—how would I perceive this event? Was getting soaked good or bad? That decision would determine the outcome for the rest of our evening. Looking at Sally, I said, "I've been baptized by the holy water! I'm gonna win tonight! I mean, what are the odds of getting soaked by one of the fountains? Hurry, let's change quickly and hit the tables!" I changed my clothes and dried my hair in record time. We ended up having an amazing evening and this is one of our favorite Vegas memories. But it all started with a choice: a choice to be happy. A choice to find the good in an event. A choice to choose humor. This event could have had the exact opposite outcome, because the event itself was neither good nor bad—it was how I viewed it that made it so.

I returned to Las Vegas in 2008, but this time with my best friend from high school, Stephanie Engnes, who lives in the Seattle area. Stephanie played ice hockey, and her team was participating in a tournament in Las Vegas. She asked me to meet her there. Her team was staying at the Monte Carlo hotel. She wanted to stay with her team, but I resisted. I will admit to being a hotel snob and I was not a fan of the Monte Carlo. But she persisted, so I agreed to stay with her and her team. The first day after we arrived, she departed to practice with her team at the local ice rink. I stayed behind and went to the spa for a massage. The spa had multiple signs that said, "Do not leave your valuables in the lockers. Use the safety deposit boxes located behind the check-in desk." Ever the rule follower, I did as instructed and handed over my wallet, phone, and room key. I removed my robe and lay down on the table naked, waiting for my massage. At that precise moment, there was a loud knock on the door to my room. A panicked manager was yelling at everyone that we needed to evacuate immediately. I pulled my robe on and, emerging from the room, I was instructed that there was no time to grab valuables, I needed to get out now. I was pushed out of the spa and into the hotel hallway. There was smoke everywhere and firemen guiding people out of the building. I was ushered out into a large parking lot. Standing there, shivering from the January cold in only a robe, I looked up to see that the top four floors of the hotel were fully engulfed in flames. I was reminded of the mass fatalities at the MGM hotel fire and realized that I didn't have my phone and couldn't call my husband and children to tell them that I was okay. I also realized in that moment that I couldn't call Stephanie—how was I going to reconnect with her? I didn't have my wallet. I had nothing. I was suddenly keenly aware of what homelessness might feel like—no phone, no money, no possessions, unsure of where I would stay, when I would eat next, or how I might connect with loved ones. In a split second, I had been stripped of everything. As Viktor Frankl noted, "Forces beyond your control can take away everything you possess except one thing, your freedom to choose how you will respond to the situation."

What then? Would I panic or become hysterical? Would this event ruin our trip? I mean, your hotel burning down is a hell of a reason to have your trip ruined. No. Again, I realized this event was neither good nor bad—it was how I chose to perceive it and how I chose to handle it that would define the outcome. I chose to remain calm. I found my way to the Las Vegas Convention Center where they were busing displaced guests. I waited there until, many hours later, Stephanie and her team arrived. They were moving guests to other MGM resorts on a first-come, first-served basis. Because I didn't have any identification or way to reach Stephanie, I had to wait for her to arrive and we were some of the last guests to be relocated—to the Luxor. We had gone from bad to worse.

We arrived at the Luxor and as we stepped into the elevator, there was a pool of vomit that I nearly stepped in. Then, it rained. While cool to look at, apparently the pyramid structure of the Luxor is prone to leaks. Water streamed into our room—through a light socket (can anyone say fire hazard?). There was so much water that they placed a bucket on our bed. We noticed that water was leaking from the windows and that the wallpaper beneath the windows was peeling off—to reveal black mold. And we had no access to our luggage or clothes. We were lucky—the fire had not damaged our floor, so we were able to retrieve our luggage the next day—but it would be two more days before I got my wallet and phone. What then? This trip was an epic fail, right? No. As horrible as it was, it was hysterical. We couldn't stop laughing. What would go wrong next? We chose humor. I was in Vegas with my best friend. I was grateful for my time with her. I borrowed money from her to buy some clothes and hit the tables. We got upgraded to a suite at the Luxor. We had fun. We made the best of our circumstances. I also learned from the entire experience. I learned that when I visit a spa, you will pry my cell phone from my cold dead hands before I leave it in a locker or a safety deposit box. I turn it off, but I keep it with me. And my phone has a pocket for my driver's license and a credit card. I plan for any possibility now. I pay attention to where the fire exit is when I stay at hotels. And when it comes to where I stay, I don't compromise. I'm willing to pay more to feel safe. Will all of this be important for me later? Maybe, or maybe by sharing this story it will save someone else from a similar hardship. Most of all, I learned that I didn't need my possessions to have fun in Vegas—I just needed friendship, a positive attitude, and a sense of adventure.

* * *

In 2016, I decided to spend my birthday in Paris with my dear friend Deb. I was beyond excited. I read books on how to dress like a Parisian woman and carefully planned out my wardrobe. I envisioned us dressed to kill, shopping at Chanel, Christian Dior, Hermes, and Louis Vuitton. I wanted to do Paris in style, so we arranged to stay at the Four Seasons Hotel George V nestled in the Golden Triangle of Paris, just off the Champs-Elysees.

As we checked into the Four Seasons, I examined the hotel. It was breathtaking. Beyond the lobby was a grand courtyard with beautiful gardens. Marble, glass, and brass gleamed everywhere. White-gloved bellmen spoke in hushed tones. This was the Paris that I had imagined.

We washed off the overseas flight and quickly changed clothes, anxious to experience Paris. On the way out, we stopped by the concierge to make dinner reservations. "What kind of cuisine do you prefer?" the concierge inquired. I explained that the scene was more important to us than the cuisine. I wanted a chic crowd and possibly a Parisian romance. "Where would be a good place to dine where two professional women could meet eligible men?" The concierge looked at us bewildered. "Je ne comprends pas," she said. I tried again, "Where could two working women meet eligible men?" The concierge's eyes grew wide with understanding. She looked startled and stunned at the same time. Deb burst out into laughter. Turning to me, she said, "She thinks we are prostitutes." OMG! My face reddened with embarrassment. Deb took over the conversation and we secured a reservation at a reputable restaurant.

Still red-faced from that exchange, I walked out the door onto the sidewalk. I was beautifully dressed, right down to my Christian Louboutin half boots with three-inch heels—ready to play my part in the story I had crafted in my head about my trip to Paris.

I could feel the white-gloved doormen watching us as we walked. I was strutting now. I was having my runway moment! As my ego grew, my heel caught a cobblestone just right, launching me into the air and propelling me forward. I was flying. Funny how when things like this happen, time really does slow down. In that split second, I realized that if I landed on my wrists or my face, I was likely to break them. So, I arched my back and threw my hands behind me in a swan dive. I held my chin up and braced for impact. I hit the sidewalk with my chest...and bounced. My breasts saved me.

I looked up from the sidewalk to see Deb, who was laughing hysterically. "Oh. My. God. You were in the air so long! You actually bounced!" she said through peals of laughter. She helped me up. As I dusted myself off, I could feel the doormen watching us. "Are you okay?" she asked. "I'm okay. My ego is bruised more than anything." "Do you want to change your shoes?" Deb asked. I did.

I did the walk of shame past the doormen as we returned to our room. Changing my shoes, I also embraced reality. This was not a Hollywood movie. Our trip would not be scripted. I had to dress for reality, not for a scene I had made up in my head.

My chest hurt, and my ego was in worse shape. By this time, I had learned that when life hits hard—or God, or the universe, whatever you'd like to call it—it was sending me a message. What then? *Stop fronting. Just be you, your authentic self*, my inner voice said. As I changed my shoes, I relaxed and let go of expectations. I refocused my attention on just enjoying my friend and experiencing Paris. I could not control what happened, but I could control my attitude. I started to laugh. It was pretty damn funny.

CHAPTER FIFTEEN

MY BODY IS NOT NORMAL

*"Speak to your body in a loving way.
It's the only one you've got. It's your home,
and it deserves your respect."*

—ISKRA LAWRENCE

It all started in elementary school. I caught my friend Christine making a V-sign with her fingers while walking behind me and then heard other kids laughing. "What were they laughing at?" I begged her. I needed to know. "Your butt," she told me. "The V-sign is because you always have panty lines." This was the Twiggy era. Women were expected to be thin and waiflike. My voluptuous bottom was not *en vogue.* Moreover, thongs were for strippers. They had not yet gone mainstream. So, I lived with my underwear perpetually creeping into a V-shape, cursed with chronic panty lines, and let's be honest—the discomfort of my underwear riding up. Ouch!

By eighth grade, I had already developed some curves and I was terribly ashamed of them. Clothes didn't fit me right. I had an hourglass figure, which meant that finding jeans was impossible—the waist was always too big and the bottom too tight. I was painfully awkward. That year for Valentine's Day, our class sold carnations for a fundraiser—for one dollar you could buy a carnation and send it to someone with a message. The carnations were delivered in homeroom. We all watched as the carnations were passed out— the popular girls and guys receiving dozens. I was ecstatic when I received one. Who was sending me a carnation? Did I have a secret admirer? I felt butterflies in my belly as I ripped open the attached message in eager anticipation. The message read: "You look like the witch from Puff-N-Stuff. Signed—The Boys in the Eighth Grade Class." A knot formed in my stomach, my cheeks flushed with heat, getting redder by the second. I could feel all eyes on me. The room began to spin as tears stung my cheeks. I sat there for a second, rereading the message in disbelief. Overwhelmed and queasy from this gut punch, I ran from the room to the bathroom, where I threw up. Wiping the vomit from my mouth, I sat back on my heels and sobbed. *All* of the boys? I was so hideous that they felt the need to let me know how ugly I was on *Valentine's Day*? Heartbroken, I wandered the halls, unsure of what to do. I eventually made my way to the principal's office and asked them to call my mother to come pick me up—I wasn't feeling well.

My parents forced me to go to school the next day. With my head down, I walked into the hallway where our lockers were located. As

I entered my lock combination, I could feel all eyes on me, burning into my back. And then, Nathan was at my side. A cute, popular boy, he leaned up against my locker, blocking me from opening it. He reached across and pushed my hair from my eyes. "Hey," he said, his voice compassionate. "Look, we all knew that Scott was going to send you that carnation, but you need to know that it wasn't from all of us." My cheeks flushed with heat again. *They all knew.* Everyone knew. Nathan's kindness helped and gradually throughout the day, Mike, Larry, Jim, and Jeff took me aside to say it was all Scott's idea and they didn't want any part of it. But the message had made its mark; my father had already told me that I wasn't beautiful. Even worse, a collective group of boys had now designated me as ugly.

I carried this mantle with me through middle school. I embraced being an ugly duckling and focused on my studies. Then, when my sister went to boarding school, I transferred to public school, which became a fresh start for me. As a junior transfer at Mariner High School, I was fresh meat, the new unknown. Leaving the library one day, I was approached by a cute guy who asked me out. I had never been on a date. Someone wanted to take me out? I asked my girlfriends what to do. "Carrie, are you an idiot? He is the quarterback on the football team! Everyone wants to go out with him!" He took me to the prom, but it didn't last. Maybe I was cute, but not cute enough? Or was it because I was a virgin who didn't put out?

We didn't have Instagram or YouTube or blowouts or fitness centers or photo filters back then. There were no tutorials or classes on how to do your makeup or style your hair. It was all trial and error—mostly error. And we didn't know what we do today about nutrition and exercise—all we knew was that we were supposed to be thin—and no matter how "skinny" I got, I still had curves. While I began to get more attention from men, I didn't trust or understand it. Someone would tell me that I was pretty, and it wouldn't stick. I would forever hear my father's voice telling me that I wasn't pretty.

My large ass continued to haunt me. I referred to it as the "White Shadow" and "the stalker." I mean, it followed me around wherever I went and wouldn't leave me alone! Could I get a restraining order against my ass?

When I was dating Jason, I got liposuction of my hips, thighs, and buttocks. I was tired of having to get everything tailored. I just wanted to be "normal." Then, after two pregnancies and breast-feeding both boys, I had a mommy makeover—a tummy tuck and a breast lift with augmentation. I was feeling better about myself, but I still needed to lose some of the baby weight.

Then, in September of 2008, I went to visit my sister, a *real* Real Housewife of Orange County. Still grappling with the death of her stepson, Tiffany was trying to create some normalcy in her life. Of course, "normal" in Orange County is not "normal" anywhere else. I took my son, Tommy, with me on this trip. Tiffany's daughter Lucy was being christened and, in true Orange County style, she was hosting a large party to celebrate at their Shady Canyon mansion. They had a gorgeous backyard overlooking a canyon, with a large pool, hot tub, and beautiful gardens. The party was catered and there were two large bouncy houses for the kids. Everyone was dressed to stop traffic. Perfect faces and perfect bodies in beautiful clothing. I was wearing a size four blue satin Betsey Johnson dress—my curves on full display—and I felt enormous in this crowd. My sister, who is six inches taller than me, was a size zero like the rest of the crowd. At five foot three, I felt short and stout.

As the party was winding down, I gathered with my sister and

Lucy's other godparents—which included a woman who owned a clothing line. Making conversation, I asked her about her designs. Tiffany interjected, "You've got to get a pair of her signature pants! They are the absolute best!" The designer shifted in her seat and, eyeing me up and down, said, "I'm not sure our sizes go that high. We only design for sizes double-zero to four." Mimicking Kate Moss's clothing line, she only designed for the super slim, and while I was a size four in Betsey Johnson, I was too big for her clothing line. I felt my cheeks redden as I stammered something about still losing the baby weight. I quickly left the group and snuck into the kitchen, gulping down a glass of wine. I had been humiliated once again in front of my sister. I was a fat embarrassment. A shame sandwich.

Tommy and I traveled back to Austin. I was miserable. I was unhappy in my marriage and filled with self-hatred. Once again, I found myself comparing myself to my sister, and I didn't measure up. All those old feelings of self-loathing resurfaced. Upon our return, I asked Jason, "Do I need to get an addiction so that I can check myself in somewhere?" I needed a break. With all that had transpired in our lives, I never had any maternity leave—not one day—and I was spent. There were simply no family members available to help out. Layer on top the dose of humiliation and shame that I had swallowed at my sister's, and I just needed to take some time to recalibrate. He knew that I was serious, so we called his sister, Heather, and she came to help Jason with the kids. So, in October of 2008, I checked myself into a week at Lake Austin Spa.

I spent that week journaling, taking exercise classes, and eating their delicious low-calorie, healthy food. I made a list of what made me happy and what was missing from my life and I emerged with a better sense of some changes that I needed in my life. Something was going on with me. I was wrestling with my life, my marriage, my career, who I was, what really mattered. Eight months later and thirty pounds lighter, I was divorced.

Later that year, speaking with my therapist, I announced, "I've been thinking. I think I have body dysmorphia!" My therapist replied, "Gee. Ya think???" We both laughed.

Since birth, I had been trained by my father that to receive love I had to live up to his ideals and do things to please him. So, I spent my life pleasing others and living up to their ideals. It never even occurred to me to consider self-acceptance and self-love—that I was lovable without DOING anything or pleasing anyone. This way of thinking was so ingrained into my psyche that it took substantial work to divorce myself from it. *I am enough? I'm worthy of love without doing anything to earn it?* Totally foreign concepts.

In 2013, I attended *Austin MD* magazine's Date-A-Doc Charity Auction at Ballet Austin's headquarters. At this event, doctors, nurses, and other medical professionals were auctioned off for dates to raise money for charity. The women who were auctioned off had very distinct body types: a runner, who was rail thin and muscular; a former pageant girl; and a curvy blonde whose face and hair resembled Jan from the Brady Bunch. I watched with anticipation as the girls were auctioned off, eager to see who would receive the highest bid. Side bets were on the former pageant girl, but the curvy Jan Brady look-alike received a bid six times higher than the runner and four times higher than the pageant girl. It wasn't even close. When "Jan" walked the catwalk, the crowd roared, and men's paddles shot into the air. I was astonished. She was clearly the crowd favorite. I could hear the men discussing how totally hot she was. What blew me away was that she did the least to look hot. She wore very little makeup, wore her hair straight, and was fit, but she was curvy…like…me? Could I be "hot"? More than anything, I realized the guys were attracted to the fact that she was comfortable in her own skin. She gave off an aura of being relaxed and happy— not high-maintenance like the pageant girl, or tightly wound like the runner. Forgive my gross stereotypes and overgeneralization, but there was an important takeaway from this event for me—men were jumping out of their chairs with excitement for a woman who loved, accepted, and embraced who she was. She was her authentic self. She didn't need to do extreme exercise, have tons of plastic surgery, or wear lots of makeup. She radiated self-confidence. This event stayed with me and has helped me through moments of comparison and self-doubt. I remind myself, *Remember who they loved best: the curvy, natural one who loved herself, was authentic, and relaxed. You don't need to try to be anything or anyone. You are lovable as you are today.*

Over the last fifteen years, as Kim Kardashian and Jennifer Lopez led the way, having a juicy booty became suddenly fashionable and body positivity became mainstream. So did thongs. Thank God.

Just as I was finally learning to love myself, Instagram exploded and so did the use of Photoshop and filters. I've had to remind myself that "comparison is the thief of joy," especially when I am comparing myself to something that isn't real. Instead, I've created a maxim for myself: "It's an Instagram world, and I'm living life unfiltered." I had a revelation recently. Much like happiness is a choice, so is self-love. When I think about getting more plastic surgery, I stop myself and say, "Or, Carrie, you could just love yourself!" Radical thought! I actually chuckle when I say this! Today, I still suffer from body dysmorphia, but I've made major progress. Today, I choose self-love. I love my body. I thank it for being healthy. I thank my thighs for helping me to walk. I express gratitude that I can move and exercise. These thighs, this ass—the bane of my existence my whole life—well, we are friends now.

CHAPTER SIXTEEN

IS HE OUT THERE?

*"Just like a shoe, if someone is meant for you,
they will fit just perfectly; no forcing,
no struggling, no pain."*

—UNKNOWN

After two divorces and many dates, I sometimes feel like Cinderella. Where is the guy who is uniquely right for me? I believe that I can learn something from each and every person whom I encounter, and the men that I date often teach me a lot. It's up to me to discover the gifts and the nuggets of wisdom from each of these encounters. With each interaction, I gain clarity on what I do and don't want. I have been on dates with all kinds of men—an NBA coach, a "billionaire," an executive at Bumble—and each of them has taught me something. When I go on these dates and it's not a fit, I thank the universe for bringing me that person and giving me greater clarity. And because I haven't met my person, my boys have never met anyone whom I have dated. I made a promise to myself after my divorce that I would keep my dating life separate and only introduce my boys to someone whom I saw as a potential future mate. That hasn't happened.

I'm impatient. I get frustrated. I get lonely. I'm ready to meet my person. Recently, I was listening to a Lewis Howes podcast. He was interviewing Mel Robbins and she said something that rocked my world: "You have to be yourself because how else are the people who are looking for you going to find you?" One of my fears with writing this book was that if I step into the light and share my story, it may scare men off. Her words reached into my soul and made me realize that I would likely meet my man *because* I was telling my story. By stepping into the light and showing my authentic self, he could find me.

It has been a long and winding road to where I am today; here are stories of some of the men that I met along the way.

THE RISING STAR

When I was practicing law, I had a client who co-founded a company that was quickly rising up the *Inc.* 500 list of the fastest growing companies in the United States. He was in his early thirties, very handsome, fit, kind, and always a gentleman. He had been voted one of Houston's most eligible bachelors. When I traveled to Houston to meet him, he would insist on picking me up and taking me to the airport. We would often have lunch or dinner together to discuss business. On one trip to Houston, he surprised me and took me to The Brownstone, then one of the top restaurants in

Houston. He knew the maître d' and had arranged for us to have the restaurant to ourselves. We were ushered to a sumptuous velvet-clad booth in a private corner. Our waiter brought us a bottle of wine. Kirk signaled for him to leave us alone. There had always been incredible sexual tension between us, but we never acted on it. I was married to Beaux. I was miserable but committed. My religious beliefs kept me from expressing how I felt.

My conversations with Kirk were always easy and I became a confidante. He valued my opinion and respected me. "Why are we here?" I asked. "What do you need to tell me?" Kirk gulped some wine down and then, twirling the base of his glass, looked at me appraisingly. "I've decided that I'm ready to get married," he said. He had recently taken out some former girlfriends, reassessing each one. It was as if he had been playing musical chairs and now the music had stopped, and he was scrambling to select the right chair. "What do you think?" he asked, staring into my eyes. His eyes told me that he wanted me to advocate for myself, but I couldn't.

"Why now?" I asked. "Because my father thinks it's time for me to settle down and start a family," he replied. Kirk had always followed the script that his father created for him. He was very concerned with doing what he perceived to be the "right" thing. There we were in this intimate setting, the sexual tension thick, both of us wanting to be with one another, but we were each concerned about what others thought. Our fear of the disapproval of others kept us apart. Instead of advocating for myself, I talked with him about the pros and cons of each girl he was considering. I wished him good luck and left The Brownstone that afternoon sad and conflicted.

A month later, as we spoke on the phone about a business matter, I told him I had news. He said that he did too. "You first," I said. "I proposed to Hope!" he said with strained enthusiasm. "We will be getting married in two months!" he continued. "What's your news?" he asked. My voice cracked as I replied with sadness, "I'm getting divorced." There was a long, awkward silence on the phone. I could hear his mind working, reflecting. After a long pause, he said, "We are sending invites out and I wanted to know your home address so that I could invite you." I felt my hope dissolve. My dreams of us together gone.

I attended his wedding at the Houstonian. He sought me out before and after the ceremony. "You look amazing," he said at the reception, giving me the once-over, with a tone of regret. I had to leave. It was just too much. So unnerved by the interaction, I wrecked my car in the parking garage. I had just watched a man whom I cared deeply about marry someone else because neither one of us could say how we really felt. We were both trapped by others' opinions, afraid to be true to ourselves.

THE DJ

After I divorced Jason, I had the housewarming party that birthed the "boob picture." I had hired a DJ to provide music for the party. My gay bestie, Mark, recommended him: "I know of someone! He is sooooo hot! Let me see if he is available!" Johnny worked the party, and my guests loved him. As he was packing up his gear later, we started chatting and learned that we had both grown up in the Seattle area and had attended rival private Christian schools—albeit about twelve years apart. Having this same shared experience, we chatted further and I learned that he had been valedictorian of his class, graduated from the University of Texas business school, and previously worked at Dell. What an unexpected surprise—the hot DJ was smart! As Johnny was saying good night, he asked if I would be open to having dinner with him sometime. I was flattered by the attention of this hot, young guy, but I didn't really see myself dating a DJ. Nevertheless, I was newly single and intrigued—there was obviously more to this guy.

We met for dinner at Uchiko where he introduced me to the—appropriately named for a first date—"Shag" sushi roll. We sat at the bar and talked. He told me about growing up in Seattle. How his love for music stemmed from car rides with his father with the radio blaring—the same father who later abandoned his family. Johnny was strikingly handsome in the James Dean kind of way and women flocked to him. He had dated all kinds of beautiful women, but he felt used, disposable. They all wanted to sleep with him, but no one took him seriously. No one saw him in full for who he was beyond his good looks. He was looking for validation. He needed to know that he was lovable. I guess we were both looking for the same thing.

He was there for me through the "boob picture" fiasco, with the much needed "Fuck them, you don't need friends like that" support. We spent Christmas together, and well, he rocked my world. He was the most honest, vulnerable man I had ever met, and I cherished that. But he was really struggling with his self-esteem; he didn't feel worthy of love.

We broke up but remained friends. As I was redoing my business website, I offered to help him create a website for his business. "Why would you do that for me?" he asked. "What are the strings?" "There are no strings," I responded. "All of the other top DJs in town have websites. You need one to grow your business." He looked at me in total disbelief. "Yes, I get that. But *why* would you do that for me? What are you expecting from me in return?" "Nothing," I said. I looked at him quizzically. "Johnny, this is what unconditional love looks like. While I don't love you romantically anymore, I love you as a friend. I want to do this for you. I expect nothing in return." We built his website and along the way he would test me, but I remained steadfast—nothing in return. I came to realize that he really needed to know that he was lovable without strings, and especially without expectation of sex.

Johnny taught me to look beyond the surface level. To peel back the layers and discover what lies beneath. He taught me not to judge or assume that a hot guy just wants to get laid. He taught me about showing up unconditionally.

THE "BILLIONAIRE"

He found me on LinkedIn and sent me a message under the guise of helping his daughter, an attorney. "My daughter is looking to move in-house, and I was wondering if you could help her?" he asked. Already suspicious of his approach, I responded, "I'm sure if your daughter is an attorney, she can advocate for herself. You are welcome to share my information with her." He came clean: "Okay, I'm not reaching out on behalf of my daughter; I just thought that you were very attractive, and I would like to meet you." After some additional conversation, I agreed to have lunch with him at the Four Seasons in Austin. He traveled to Austin just for our lunch. He told me about his life and that one of his close friends was Wayne Huizenga, former owner of the Miami Dolphins. I enjoyed the conversation, but I wasn't feeling any attraction. In fact, the opposite;

he was really full of himself, and this was a huge turnoff for me. At the end of our lunch, he said, "So if I buy a place in Austin, will you agree to see me three times a week?" Of course, my quick wit voiced a thought: *What's in it for me?* I was shocked and offended by his proposal and told him so. "What kind of girl do you think I am?" I thanked him for lunch and bid him adieu.

Our interaction was affirming for me. I care about *who* someone is and what they stand for—their character and values. I want a man whom I can respect and admire, and professional success is part of that, but I have never dated someone because of the size of their wallet, and this interaction affirmed that.

THE TRADER

It was November 2012 and Austin hosted its first-ever Formula One race. People from around the world descended on Austin to experience this epic event. I went to the W Hotel with a group of friends to attend an opening party. As I walked into the Living Room, I was surrounded by a sea of men. The hotel lounge was packed. I overheard a group of local guys complaining, "I hate the way these Italian guys think they can just take our women." As he finished his sentence, my eyes locked on a tall, muscular, handsome guy pushing the local guys to the side and reaching for me. He slid his arm through the pack of men and around my waist, pulling me toward him. "Hi! You are the prettiest girl in the room! I had to meet you!" I laughed out loud at what had just occurred. I loved how self-assured this guy was. He had my full attention. "I'm Michael. People call me Mac. Look, I've got to run and meet my friends, but I will be back in fifteen minutes." He walked me to a couch and settled me in with a drink. "Do not go anywhere!" he commanded as he walked away, keeping his eyes on me.

True to his word, he was back in a few minutes. I learned that he was a trader from New York. He had grown up in Greenwich, Connecticut, the son of a very successful attorney. His father, whom he adored, had passed away recently. He was in town for Formula One and staying with his best friend, who split time between Greenwich and Austin. We spent the weekend together. I loved the way that he treated me. He knew how to take care of a woman. He made me feel like a queen.

He explained to me why he had a lion tattoo on his shoulder. It was there to cover his fraternity tattoo. He wanted to forget his painful past. Along with another fraternity brother, he had been accused of rape. The victim never filed a complaint, and no charges were ever brought, but since Mac was the quarterback of the football team, the event was high-profile and the school acted quickly to dismiss him without hearing his side. He sued the school and was reinstated, but the damage had been done. Mac transferred schools and his football career was over. He made a career for himself on Wall Street and put his past in the rearview mirror. His story stirred up all kinds of emotions in me because of my experience with being raped in college. I hadn't reported it because I feared being vilified. Here I was facing someone who had been wrongly accused. I heard his pain. I appreciated his honesty and vulnerability. We were united in trying to forget these past experiences and move on and live life to the fullest.

We said our goodbyes and he disappeared from my life, other than running into each other once when I was on a trip to Soho. I knew he wasn't my person, but I loved that he knew what he wanted.

I loved that he was so confident in choosing me. I loved how I felt when I was with him. I looked for those qualities in the other men I met. Then, about a year later, I opened *People* magazine and there he was. "Bethenny Frankel dating Michael A. Cerussi III." I felt a mixture of jealousy, envy, and admiration. They looked happy together. I admire Bethenny—she is scrappy, entrepreneurial, and big-hearted, with a wicked sense of humor. I could understand how he could be good for her during her very public and messy divorce. Mac has a way of shutting out the rest of the world and making you feel protected and that you are all that matters. I mentally cheered them on and was sad to hear when their relationship had ended.

THE TECH EXECUTIVE

I was set up on a blind date with a local tech executive. He was working for one of the hottest companies in Austin at the time, soon to go public. We met for a drink at Three Forks. I walked in and the chemistry was instant. He stood to introduce himself. Thrusting his hand forward, he said, "Hi, Mark, I'm Carrie." We both chuckled at his nervous blunder. "I mean I'm Mark! Nice to meet you, Carrie." His cheeks reddened as his eyes took me in. Conversation was easy and the wine flowed. I was intrigued by his intelligence and ambition. I thought this could be my man.

A week later, he picked me up in his Porsche convertible and took me to Uchiko. Our dinner was magical and things progressed. Our work schedules were crazy so, while not ideal, we agreed our next date would be on Mother's Day. I would get a sitter and we would meet after my boys were in bed. We agreed to meet at Olive & June, a contemporary Italian restaurant built around a garden terrace. I found a spot at the bar and ordered myself a drink. It was getting late, and I realized that I hadn't heard from Mark. I shot him a text inquiring what his ETA was. No reply. My cheeks began to redden as the bartender watched me quizzically. An hour had passed and I was into my second drink, with still no word from Mark. Was this really happening to me? Was I being stood up on Mother's Day? As I finished my second drink, tears began to sting my cheeks. Yes, this was really happening to me. Embarrassed and angry, I went to pay for my check, but the bartender felt badly for me. Drinks were on the house. I made my way home, embarrassed to face my babysitter and explain why I was home so early. What a shitty Mother's Day. Anger welled up as I thought about my mother at the end stages of her disease, of the time I had spent getting ready, the money I had paid my babysitter, the precious time wasted.

Eventually, I heard from Mark; one of their employees had died and he had flown to his hometown to attend the funeral and speak on behalf of the company. He explained what a hard day it had been on him. Could he have let me know sooner? Could he have thought about me and my feelings? Could he have apologized and sent flowers because he couldn't make it? Of course, but he didn't. By now, you are screaming the obvious—that he was a narcissist—but I was coming from a place of lack, so I chose to buy into his story. We met for breakfast a few days later. He explained to me that I just had to understand that he was a busy guy and had a crazy schedule, and it was part of the deal. So a pattern developed, because yes, you teach people how to treat you, and I had agreed that his behavior was okay. He stood me up two more times, each time more painful than the last.

When I met Mark, with our instant chemistry and rapport, I

had envisioned us as a power couple. I had created a story in my head that I wanted to believe. I kept chasing that false dream, disregarding how he was treating me. Maya Angelou famously said, "When someone shows you who they are, believe them the first time." I have learned to take this advice to heart. Now, if someone cancels on me or stands me up, they don't get a second chance. I am clear that I want a man who can't wait to see me. He should be concerned with me and my feelings—if he is not, this is a neon light flashing to run.

The best thing that came out of my experience with Mark? Sitting there on that barstool waiting for him on Mother's Day, I thought about all of the other single mothers out there who had suffered similar experiences. Not having any family available to step in and help with childcare, I had never had a single hour of free babysitting. I thought about my friends who complained that their parents didn't help out enough. I realized that people don't know what they have, and what others don't. I thought about other single moms who just needed a break, a hand up, a day off. That Mother's Day a seed was planted: that was the day that the idea for the Blooming Foundation was born. A foundation to give women, especially single moms, a hand up.

THE RUNNER

I was walking on the trail along Lady Bird Lake in Austin. It was odd, I felt like I needed to take a different route—that I might meet someone. I crossed over to the south side of the lake and proceeded west toward Mopac. As I crossed the bridge over Barton Springs, a handsome man ran toward me. He wore a T-shirt with a picture of Africa and the word "Hope" inside of it. Time slowed as we passed one another exchanging smiles. He was cute. I turned to watch him run past and continued walking, finally stopping at a stone terrace overlooking the lake. It had become my practice to stop at the beautiful overlooks along the lake and take a moment of gratitude before continuing on my walk. As I paused and gave thanks that I live in such a beautiful city, I pulled out my phone to check a message. I heard footsteps approaching and glanced up. The handsome jogger was standing in front of me. He had run back to see me. He asked for my phone and, flabbergasted, I handed it to him. He entered his phone number and ran off. I glanced down at my phone. There was a number but no name. "Wait!" I called after him, "What's your name?" In an instant, I fired off a text message. "Hi, I'm Carrie. I was hoping you would come back! I wanted to meet you!" About an hour later, he responded, "I about had a heart attack! I've never done that before! But I felt like I needed to meet you!" This was what I had been waiting for. A guy who literally ran back to meet me. Someone who recognized my beauty and ran toward me. Someone who couldn't wait to see me. Isn't that what every girl wants? Don't we deserve that?

Yet, it was not to be. As amazing as this story is, he turned out to be married. Unhappily married, he said, in the process of separation—two marriage counselors and two years of no sex later, he was waiting for COVID to end to move out. We met and walked one morning. We walked seven miles—which was torture for him, a runner. As we walked, I listened to his story, to the description of his loveless marriage. I wanted to believe him. But part of me didn't. Ninety-five percent of that first conversation was him selling me, painting a picture that I would buy into. But my intuition nagged at me: too many details is a red flag for deception. His explanation was too detailed and long—about six miles too long. There was definitely an attraction, but he was unconcerned with "me" beyond my physical body. He didn't seem to care about my work, my children, the book I was writing, or any aspect of my life, really. Including my boundaries. Nagging alarm bells were going off: *He's lying to you, he's a narcissist.* I tried to quiet them. I tried bargaining with the universe: *I'm so tired of holding out for the "one." Can't I lower my standards just for Thanksgiving and Christmas? Can't I just put my blinders on and have hot, steamy sex with this guy during COVID? I'm tired of being alone. I need to be TOUCHED!*

But I was in the flow. My life was taking off. I didn't want to do anything to sidetrack me from that. As I struggled with my emotions, he canceled plans to meet. And then I knew. A wave of grief overwhelmed me. It was not to be. I deserved better and I knew it. I was attempting to sell myself short, but the universe had conspired and said "no." It told me that I was staying in flow and not compromising my standards. I deserve the whole enchilada—not a partial, sad bite.

I wanted to believe in the story. It was a great romantic beginning! I need to stop believing in the story. I need to believe in me. It's not always fun or easy. But he is out there, I know it.

THE CMO

We met on Bumble. His profile said, "CMO at consumer technology company." He was tall, athletic, and handsome. Totally my type! I swiped right. He was from New Zealand and had lived all over the world. We arranged to have drinks at the Garage Bar in Austin.

The attraction was instant. That kind of chemical reaction that is one in a million. I touched his arm and felt electricity pulsate through my body. I was enthralled. He captivated me. The conversation was easy and the attraction strong.

He was new to his company and in the process of moving to Austin. He still had a home in Los Angeles and would commute home on the weekends. When in Austin, he stayed at the Proper Hotel, a swanky downtown establishment frequented by the "in" crowd. I was enchanted, and the relationship progressed.

Then COVID hit, and he was stuck in LA.

His company's CEO was talking about moving the company headquarters from Austin to Dallas. He was adamant that he wasn't moving to Dallas. He parted ways with the company and no longer had a tie to Austin.

We texted frequently, but he was reluctant to talk on the phone, Facetime, or do virtual dates. I would try to end things because it hurt not to see him, but our text exchanges were like crack cocaine—highly addictive and "feel-good." But that's all that they were—just words.

"Love is not a feeling. It is an action. Love is what love does," I told him, quoting from Steven Covey's *The Road Less Traveled*. His words felt so good, but without the actions to back them up, they were meaningless.

Then, in December, after nine months of texting without seeing him, I went to dinner with a friend. She brought her boyfriend along. They met in Nantucket in September. He lives in New York and travels to Austin every other week just to see her. Listening to their story, it was like a slap in the face. A wake-up call. What the hell was I doing, settling for scraps? I was so happy for them, and

I knew what I had to do.

I texted him, "I cherish our interactions. But you aren't invest-ing in me or us and that hurts. I don't want to, but I need to let you go so that I can move on and open my head and my heart to someone who wants to invest in a future with me. You are such an amazing man...if you can get there, hit me up, but if not, let me go."

A month later, we reconnected and started having Zoom calls on a weekly basis. During our regular chats, he never made an offer to come see me. Meanwhile, I kept hearing the song "If the World Was Ending" by Julia Michaels and JP Saxe on the radio, and the words nagged at me. We had been living through a pandemic. In a sense, the world as we knew it was ending. If he didn't have a sense of urgency to come see me now, when would he ever?

I knew what I had to do. I said, "Goodbye."

He had kept telling me that the timing was just off. But I didn't want to hear it—he checked all the boxes! Except for one very big box: showing up for me, wanting to spend time with me. He was going through some changes in his life, and like many of us, wanted things to line up perfectly before he would feel worthy to be in a relationship. I kept telling him that he was perfect the way that he was and that he didn't need to change a thing, but he couldn't believe that. And as is often the case, life is like a mirror—we have to observe someone else's behavior to recognize it in ourselves. I realized that for many years, I had been guilty of the same thing. I am enough. I am worthy of love as I am, today. These are my daily affirmations.

THE HEDGE FUND GUY

We met on Hinge. He had relocated from Greenwich, Connecticut, to Austin to start a hedge fund. Our first date was at Aba. On this date, my primary concern was to determine if this guy was an arrogant asshole or not. I entered the date with a preconceived bias against hedge fund guys based entirely on their portrayal in the media. He surprised me. He was very low-key and kind, but with a quirky sense of humor. He was extremely fit, which I loved. Then he announced that he was a pescatarian, which I did not love. The conversation was easy, so we agreed to another date. This time, after dinner at Peacock, we ended up at his place. I noticed that he had a number of familiar books on his kitchen countertop: Dale Carnegie's *How to Make Friends and Influence People*, Gary Chapman's *The Five Love Languages*, and Daniel Goleman's *Emotional Intelligence*. "These are great books!" I said. "I read them every year," he explained. This gave me pause. Having read these books myself, I immediately understood and absorbed their teachings. I couldn't imagine the need to reread them every year. Our conversation turned to *The Five Love Languages*. "What's your love language?" I asked. He replied, "Quality time and acts of service." He didn't ask, so I volunteered, "Over the last few years, I have come to realize that my primary love language is words of affirmation." He grunted a reply (which I interpreted as he thought my love language was weak). The conversation turned back to him as he showed me around his kitchen and talked to me about his diet and his workouts. As the evening was coming to an end, I started to reflect and realized that he had never paid me a single compliment. Even after I had told him what my love language was—nothing. An emotionally intelligent man would have immediately responded with a flirty compliment. Now I knew why he reread those books every year: he clearly needed the reminders. Interpersonal skills were not his strength.

While he was driving me home, he continued to talk about his diet and how he now looked the best that he ever had. Turning to me, he said, "Now we've got to work on you!" *What did he just say to me? Did he really just say that?* I told him that my love language was words of affirmation, and instead of paying me a compliment he says, "Now, we've got to work on you"? *Wow. Just wow*, I thought. I went to sleep that night and had nightmares about him. I was trying to escape him. He was my father. He was Jason. My love language is words of affirmation not because I am weak but because I have spent a lifetime with men who not only did not give compliments but also regularly made digs at me. Oftentimes in the guise of a joke, but the effect was the same. I was crystal clear on one thing: I'd had enough of that. I do not want, and will not allow myself, to partner with a man like that. I need a man who lifts me up and is supportive of me. He kept texting me to go out again. I ignored his texts for weeks but finally responded that we weren't a match. I thanked God again for giving me more clarity. I don't care who you are—no one gets to talk to me like that.

CHAPTER SEVENTEEN

DEFINING MOMENTS

*"The question of what we are can only be answered
by ourselves. We each decide what we are by the life choices
we make. How we were made, who are parents are, where
we are from, the color of our skin, who we choose to
love, all those things do not define us. Our actions define
us and will keep defining us until even after death."*

—P. C. CAST

Most of the time, we fumble through life not cognizant of our impact on others or that we are in the middle of a defining moment. But on occasion, a situation confronts us that is so obviously a defining moment it is like a neon sign blinking brightly saying, "Choose carefully—this is important." When I was in law school, I encountered such a moment.

THE GOOD SAMARITAN

One night after drinking in the French Quarter with my law school friend Mary, I was driving on St. Charles Avenue headed toward the Warehouse District, where Mary lived in a gorgeous loft across the street from Emeril's Restaurant. As we drove down St. Charles Avenue, the street was empty except for a large lump in the middle of the road. As we got closer, I realized that it was a man who had been beaten and was covered in blood. "Oh my God, that's a man in the road!" I exclaimed. I pulled up next to him, blocking the road so that he wouldn't get hit by oncoming traffic. Mary started to panic. "What are you doing?" she asked tersely. Within seconds of seeing him, I knew that this was a test. This was exactly like the parable of the Good Samaritan in the Bible. I also knew that if I read in the newspaper the next day that the man we had seen had died or been run over by a car because we hadn't stopped, I wouldn't be able to live with myself. "We need to move him out of the road!" I replied. "No way! It's too dangerous! We need to get out of here in case whoever beat him comes back!" Mary exclaimed in a panic. The year was 1992 and we didn't have cell phones. We couldn't simply call the cops and block traffic until they arrived. It was up to us.

Mary and I dragged the bloody, unconscious man across the road and onto the sidewalk, then we jumped into my car and drove to her apartment to call 911. We drove back to the scene so that we could flag down the police and make sure that the man got the attention that he needed. As we approached him again, a car was pulling up next to him and four huge men got out and approached him with a tire iron. I pulled up behind them. Mary was screaming at me now: "What the fuck are you doing? Oh my God, they are going to finish him off!" I am not sure what possessed me, but my body filled with adrenalin and this little five-foot-three, 120-pound blonde girl opened her car door and stepped out into the road and started to scream at these men, "Get the FUCK away from him! We've called the cops and they are on their way! They'll be here any second!" Mary was cowering in her seat trying to shrink from view. The men looked at me, exchanged a few words and got back into their car and left. The police and EMS arrived shortly thereafter and took the man to the hospital. As all of this happened, I had total awareness that I was being tested and I learned that I had the courage to make the right choice. My character was being tested. Who was I? What I loved about this moment was that the decision was so easy. I had total clarity. The decision to stop and help was the only right decision for me. I learned something about myself that day. I learned who I was, what I stood for, and what I was capable of when I was confident in my action. I was someone who stopped to help. I was someone who took action instead of ignoring a problem. I lived my values. My actions matched my beliefs. As the great John Wooden once said, "Be more concerned with your character than your reputation, because your character is what you really are, while your reputation is merely what others think you are…the true test of a man's character is what he does when no one is watching."

SAYING NO TO RACISM

My first husband, Beaux, grew up in Metairie, Louisiana, a suburb of New Orleans. His family still lived there, so we would occasionally make the drive from Austin to New Orleans and stay with his parents. On one particular trip in 1994, we spent some time with his parents and then headed to the French Quarter so Beaux could see friends and former work colleagues. We stopped for lunch at a beautiful restaurant with a second-floor outdoor terrace that gave us a view of the crowd below. The waitstaff was comprised of older Black men in white tuxedo jackets who practiced politeness, deference, and "yes sir, no sir." The service was particularly slow this day, and Beaux was getting agitated. He was rude to our waiter and started to refer to him using the N-word. The more agitated and ruder Beaux became, the more my blood pressure rose. The more uncomfortable that I became, the louder Beaux became and the more he threw around the N-word. I'd had it. I was totally embarrassed and ashamed that I was married to this bigot. "If you use the N-word one more time, I am walking out of this restaurant!" I told Beaux. "You will not! Where are you going to go?" Beaux pushed back. Then he unleashed another racist rant, and as the N-word left his lips, I pushed my chair back, walked down the stairs, hailed a taxi to the airport, and flew home to Austin—leaving my suitcase, my car, and my husband behind. I acted with total clarity and conviction. I had voted with my feet.

He was furious. I had embarrassed him in front of his family. He had to explain to his parents why I had abandoned him in New Orleans. I didn't care. I was done. He in no way reflected who I was or what I stood for. In fact, he stood for what I despised. I didn't want to be alone, but I could not be around someone who spewed such vile hatred and ignorance. This moment gave me clarity about who I was and what I stood for. I would rather be alone than be with a racist. Later life lessons taught me that more was required of me than walking away. I needed to be affirmatively antiracist. Now, I seek to understand and elevate others from different races and backgrounds. Diversity has become a passion. What a wonderful gift to receive from such a horrible experience.

MAKING A DIFFERENCE
BEHIND THE SCENES

After I became an executive search professional focused on attorneys, I worked on a General Counsel search for one of the subsidiaries of a Fortune 500 company. I had successfully completed numerous searches for this company and had earned the trust of the Chief Legal Officer. The company made an offer to a white male, who declined the offer. This was a surprise to everyone. I had to restart the search and submitted an entirely new slate of candidates. The candidate receiving the job offer this time was an African American female. Typically, the company determines the offer, and the offer is conveyed by me to the candidate. For some reason, the company extended the offer to the candidate directly, leaving me out of the loop. I called their head of executive recruiting to discuss what had happened. She told me that the offer had been extended and what the terms of the offer were. I started to panic. The compensation package offered to the African American female was less than that offered to the white male who had declined the offer. I asked the head of executive recruiting, "Did the CLO sign off on this? Was he aware that the offer was lower?" She replied, "Yes, he signed off on it. I don't know if he realized that it was lower or not. We were all surprised that he approved it." Wow. They let the CLO sign off on it without pointing out the discrepancy. This needed to be fixed immediately, for two reasons: it was important that the African American female be paid the same as the white male, but also because I believed that this was unintentional and could potentially be harmful to the CLO's career. I called the CLO's executive assistant. She told me that he was on vacation in the Caribbean. I told her that it was time-sensitive and important. She gave me his cell phone number. I reached him in the Caribbean and told him about the discrepancy in the compensation. He thanked me for calling him and asked if the candidate had accepted the offer yet. She had not. He said, "Call her and tell her we really want her and increase her offer." Which is exactly what I did. She accepted the offer, never knowing what had happened behind the scenes.

I took a great risk when I reached out to the CLO, disturbing him on his vacation. If the discrepancy was intentional, that could have ended my relationship with the company. However, I trusted my belief that the CLO's approval of the offer was an oversight, and that he would never have knowingly discriminated against an African American or female candidate. His response demonstrated that I was right. I easily could have said nothing. But I couldn't say nothing; my personal convictions and sense of fairness demanded that I act. By standing up for what I believed in, it actually strengthened my relationship with the company. I had earned their trust.

NOT SO SUPER BOWL

It was January of 2005. I was in the third trimester of my second pregnancy, working, and taking care of a toddler. Every year since we had met, Jason and I would throw a Super Bowl party. It was our big party of the year and we would go all out, setting up a bar by our pool with food stations around our house. This was our signature event and our friends looked forward to it every year. This year, a week before the party, I developed chronic diarrhea. I tried to ignore it and drink lots of fluids, but it just kept getting worse. My doctor insisted that I be admitted to the hospital for IV fluids and monitoring.

At the hospital, they took a urine sample, and my urine was dark brown. I was terrified. This was a very bad sign. My body was in ketosis, which could be harmful to the baby. They needed to get fluids into me quickly to protect the baby. The hospital was busy and there wasn't a normal room for me, so I was hooked up to an IV and left in a delivery room. I felt the cool, crisp hospital gown cold against my body. The bed, designed to enable childbirth, was stiff and uncomfortable. The television didn't work, so I was left to stare at the walls of the room and ponder my circumstances. Jason and I didn't have much family and we had no family nearby. Tears welled up in my eyes. I wanted my mom. I wanted Jason's mom. But Jason's mom was dead, and my mom was mentally incapacitated. There was no one there to comfort me.

After arranging for care for our younger son, Tommy, Jason came to visit me in the hospital. He was agitated. He paced the room. "Why did you have to do this now?" he asked. "Couldn't this have waited? This is totally going to fuck up our Super Bowl party," he continued. He was furious with me. "I don't have control over my body," I replied. "What am I supposed to do?" I felt guilty. Jason had been through so much in the past few years. I didn't want to do anything that caused him more grief. I knew that the Super Bowl party was something that he looked forward to every year. I wanted to bring him that happiness. As he stood there glowering at me, I did what many of us women do. I resolved to put my needs on hold to please him, just like my mother had. I checked myself out of the hospital so that the Super Bowl party could go on as planned. I checked myself back into the hospital after the party and then got IV fluids at home for another week.

I had made him happy, but at what cost? I resented the hell out of him. His fucking Super Bowl party was more important than my health and the health of our baby? How dare he prioritize a party over us! But I lived in fear of his anger. I was walking on eggshells with him, afraid that my actions would set him off. I was suddenly transported back to my childhood, tiptoeing around, trying to keep everything copacetic. I had fallen back into a similar pattern of giving up myself, my very real physical needs, in order to keep everyone happy.

Then, after Andy was born and his baby teeth came in, we noticed a brown-tinged mark on one of his front teeth. It was gradually getting bigger and had developed into a sizeable hole. I asked the dentist about it. "Were you sick during your third trimester?" he asked. "That's when baby teeth are developed in utero." His words were like a gut punch. A gut punch that would forever change my behavior. I *had* been sick, and my baby son's smile bore the consequences of it. I felt rage, then guilt. I thought of all of the times that my mother was so focused on pleasing my father that we had been neglected. I was behaving like my mother. By focusing on pleasing Jason, I hadn't just hurt myself, my child had been harmed too. My heart broke for Andy. This toxic pattern had to end. I resolved to take care of myself and my children first. Priorities over parties. Self-care over pleasing others.

HARD-HEADED

When I was done having children, I decided to have endometrial ablation done so that I would no longer get my period. I mean, what's the point of dealing with that monthly drama if I didn't have to? My doctor prescribed some medication for me to take the night before the procedure. He told me that it would make the procedure go more smoothly. I took the medication and went to sleep.

I woke up about an hour later needing to use the bathroom. I got out of bed and walked into the master bathroom and the next thing I knew, I woke up on the bathroom floor. The floor was cold and my head hurt. I reached up to feel my head and felt blood and sharp pieces of tile in my hair. We had just redone our bathroom with a beautiful mosaic tile floor—which had an incredible meat-tenderizing effect on my head. My skull was mush. I knew that I needed to get help, so I grabbed hold of the sink cabinet and hoisted myself up. Then, I woke up on the floor again. Was this Groundhog Day? I was so confused. I crawled to the sink cabinet again and pulled myself up. Only to wake up on the floor again. Was this a dream? I was starting to feel crazy. What the hell was going on with me? I reached my hand to my head again and felt the warm, sticky blood and sharp pieces of tile mashed into my hair and scalp. I lay there for a while feeling the cold of the tiles, unsure of what to do. I felt numb. The house was silent. I felt totally and utterly alone. I was reminded of that saying, "If a tree falls in a forest and no one is around to hear it, is there a sound?" I was the tree and my house was the forest. No one heard me.

I lay there for a while longer contemplating my options. Our house was so big there was no point in screaming. No one would hear. The boys were upstairs in their rooms asleep, and Jason was asleep on the couch in the kids' playroom at the other end of the house. I now fully understood the meaning of hard-headed. It took me three attempts to absorb the fact that standing was not a good plan. My head was throbbing now, so I rolled over and crawled to the toilet closet where there was a phone. I called 911 and they instructed me that someone was going to have to let them into the house. I crawled into the bedroom, down the hallway past the study and into the living room. Everyone was still asleep.

Reaching from my knees, I let the paramedics into our home. Immediately, they wanted to make sure that I hadn't been beaten. Was my husband at home? I told them where to find Jason and explained that the children were asleep upstairs. They woke Jason up and explained what had happened. They were transporting me to the hospital. Jason would follow once he had arranged for childcare.

At the emergency room, they explained that the medication I had taken had caused my blood pressure to drop, which was why I kept fainting. They cleaned my wound and stapled my head—twelve staples in all. Each staple made me wince with pain. Pain that I welcomed. Pain made me feel. I realized lying there on the cold tile floor how numb I had become in my marriage and in my home. I was living in a cold mausoleum. The house that we had spent seven years renovating meant nothing without love in our marriage. Had I fallen in a different direction—perhaps hit my head on the corner of the sink—I could have died, and no one would have heard. This thought sent chills through me. As I reflected on all of this, I realized that having a big home and a lot of stuff didn't matter to me anymore. I just wanted to feel. I wanted to feel loved.

THE GRATITUDE PROJECT

My sweet friend Megan had a rough start in the legal profession. At the first firm where she had worked, one of the partners started masturbating in front of her. She reported him and nothing happened. She changed firms and her new firm was struggling financially. We talked about her career and where she wanted to end up. She confided in me that she really wanted to switch from commercial litigation to family law. I encouraged her to make the switch. The problem was that she had become incredibly negative. She was down on herself and the legal profession. And because of her circumstances, she had developed a negative outlook on life. Whenever I would see her, it was constant complaining. Which, let's be honest, was getting very old.

Then I had an idea! "Megan, let's do a project together," I suggested. "For the next thirty days, why don't we both commit to performing one act of service and one statement of gratitude every day. We will hold one another accountable. What do you think?" We discussed what constituted an "act of service" and decided that we would count time spent on philanthropic endeavors that we were already involved in, doing things for others, even giving up a parking space or opening a door for someone who needed assistance. Part of this exercise taught us to acknowledge what we were already doing, but it also made us raise our game. We had reached an agreement.

We approached our project with a sense of excitement. For the month of January, I volunteered with local philanthropies, did my friend's dishes, practiced random acts of kindness, and was actively looking for things that I could do for others. We would report our acts of service to one another, give our statement of gratitude, and offer encouragement and support to one another.

At the end of the month, a miraculous shift had happened. Megan had her dream job working with one of the preeminent divorce attorneys in Dallas. She became positive and hopeful again. Her life had transformed. And so had mine. My mindset had shifted. I became more positive and hopeful, too. I felt an incredible sense of gratitude for my life and my friendships. I felt the world open up to me. And today, Megan is one of the most highly respected and sought-after divorce attorneys in Dallas. She is positive and supportive. A beacon of light to her clients. Through this exercise, we both learned that through the daily practice of shifting our mindset from focusing on the negative things in our lives to gratitude and what we could do for others, our view of the world changed. This shift was powerful and dramatic. Not only did it make me feel better, but people began to respond to me differently. The more that I gave and expressed gratitude, the more I received the same in return. My positive daily interactions with others improved my mood. It was like a feedback loop. Today, I continue this daily practice of expressing gratitude and looking for ways to positively impact others. There has been a grand shift in my life. My attitude has attracted more positive, loving people into my life, and I experience joy on a more regular basis.

ON BEING PRESENT

In July of 2011, I took a trip to Italy with my friend Tasha. We flew into Milan and drove to Lake Como, took a train to Rome, hired a car to drive us down the Amalfi Coast, and then we took a boat to the Isle of Capri. The landscape was breathtaking, the weather was perfect, the sun sparkled off the sea. All the while, Tasha was texting a guy she really liked. Our first night on Capri, they exchanged nearly ninety texts. We were in Capri in July! There was so much beauty to see, and the people-watching was epic! But I was growing frustrated with my friend; her face was always in her phone. She had traveled all the way to Italy, but she wasn't experiencing it. Her head and her heart were elsewhere. I begged her to put her phone away. On our second evening in Capri, she acquiesced. With her phone hidden away, and her beautiful energy radiating outward, magic happened.

We went to a local bar and started chatting with an American couple. They were beautiful, high energy, charismatic, gracious, and fun. I quickly learned that I had a friend in common with the gentleman. I shot our mutual friend a Facebook message, and learned that we were hanging out with Billy Miller from *The Young and the Restless*. His travel companion was Chrishell Stause, then of *All My Children*, more recently of *Selling Sunset* and *Dancing with the Stars*. They invited us to join them at another, exclusive, club. We drank and danced into the early morning hours and thanked them for the best night of our trip.

A few days later we returned to Rome, and as we were walking by the Spanish Steps, we realized that Chrishell and Billy were walking in front of us. We ended up spending another evening together. But none of this would have happened if we had our faces in our phones. There were so many exciting things happening around us that we would have missed. Our time hanging out with Billy and Chrishell was the highlight of our trip. What else would we have missed out on having our heads down? How many incredible people did we walk by without stopping to chat or learn about them?

Chrishell and Billy are inspiring not because they are actors, but because of their stories—the challenges they've overcome, the hidden successes they shared with us. Our two evenings with them were gifts. They inspired and energized us, but also opened our eyes to the magic and opportunities around us if we just keep our heads up and are present in this miracle called life.

Each of these stories was a defining moment for me. Together, they are part of the fabric of who I am. In some of these stories, it was a choice I made that defined me. In others, it was how I chose to respond to something that happened to me. As I have learned so well, if the universe is trying to teach me a lesson, it will keep on serving up the same thing until I get the message. Sometimes I recognize the lesson quickly. Other times, it takes something more dramatic—like cracking my head—to finally get the message and change my behavior. The key is to be regularly looking for the lessons in life and learning from others' life experiences. In a famous story told about Warren Buffett, a man says to Buffett, "It was a failure, but I learned my lesson." To which Buffett replied, "The trick is to avoid expensive lessons and to learn from the stories of others."

CHAPTER EIGHTEEN

MIDLIFE REDIRECTION

*"Ultimately, man should not ask what the meaning
of his life is, but rather must recognize that it is he who is asked.
In a word, each man is questioned by life; and he can only
answer to life by answering for his own life; to life
he can only respond by being responsible."*

—VIKTOR FRANKL

In the wake of losing my mother and watching Stephanie Woodard decline, my business began to dry up. My biggest client stopped sending me work. I knew that the company was dealing with massive changes, but it was hard not to take it personally, and the steep drop in income could not have come at a worse time. I started seeing a life coach and exploring different careers. I was defeated and depressed and felt like I was swimming through muck.

The life coach was a disaster—he was self-motivated and always looking for an angle for himself. He encouraged me to take a stab at starting an app. It was the business du jour and I devoted a year of my time and thousands of dollars to the endeavor. I will never forget attending a local Women in Technology event at Capital Factory in Austin. The female CEO of a hot Austin company, whom I thought was my friend, was one of the speakers. I sought her out after the event concluded. She asked me what I was up to and I told her about my app. "I'm working on a startup," I told her. "What you have is an idea, not a startup!" she replied, dismissing me before walking away. I stood there stunned. This "friend" had been profiled by the local magazines and business journals as helping other women. Her words cut like a knife. I never felt so small.

I had incorporated my business, put together an advisory board, issued advisor shares, completed financial modeling, hired front- and back-end developers, commissioned a UX consultant, determined branding, registered a trademark, filed a patent application, determined how to seed the app with users, figured out the customer journey, put together a pitch deck, and started to raise money. She didn't ask about the details. She simply dismissed me. In the end, I decided that I was not the right person to take the app to market. The app was a heavy lift and outside of my area of expertise. But as fate would have it, my legal recruiting business revived.

I view this time period as being lost in the wilderness. I was looking for something and I didn't even know what. I felt an urgency to achieve something so that my life mattered. The world— Instagram, social media, the news—promoted the message that in order to matter, you had to achieve, acquire, or appear a certain way. But the more I pursued this way of life, the unhappier I became.

Then in 2016, I went to a medical spa to get an IPL Photofacial. The laser procedure went horribly wrong, and I was left with second- and third-degree burns on my face, neck, décolleté, and shoulders. I developed a secondary bacterial infection and then a systemic yeast infection from the steroids and antibiotics I was given. I looked like a monster and the yeast infection left me with terrible brain fog. I would wake up in the morning and go sit on the couch to have my coffee, then hours later discover that I had spent the entire day staring at the wall. My hair began to fall out in large clumps. It took months for the doctors to correctly diagnose the secondary yeast infection. During this time, I was essentially catatonic and nonfunctioning. I had suffered a severe trauma and to fix the scars, I had to undergo fractional laser treatments with platelet-rich plasma. Basically, every four weeks for six months, the affected areas would be reduced to mush and covered with my own blood. I suffered from PTSD from the original laser treatment, so they would have to give me Xanax or Valium to do the treatment. Even then, I would wail throughout. The scar tissue was so bad that my nose twisted and my neck sagged. This required a nose job and a neck lift. I had to sue the med spa to cover the cost of my treatments.

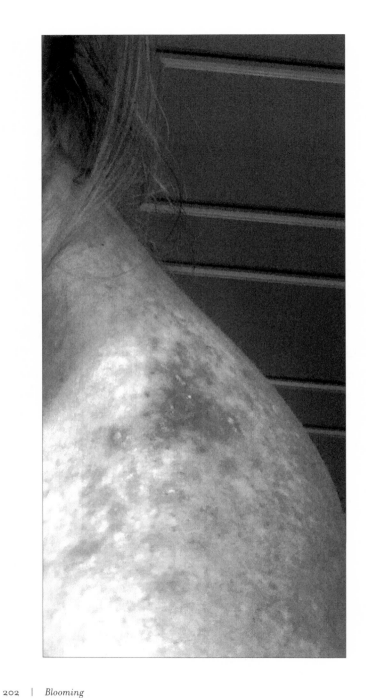

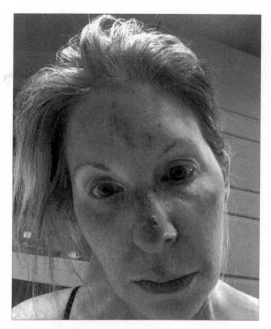

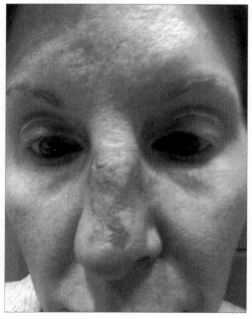

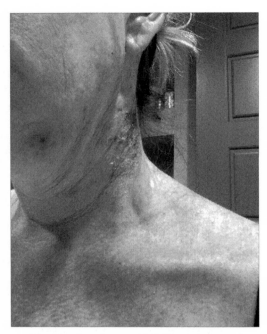

Who knew that a laser could do this much damage?

Needless to say, the laser treatment had scorched not just my skin, but my spirit and my livelihood. I had been taken down to nothing. The settlement from the lawsuit didn't come close to covering the costs to repair the damage or the lost income. I went through hundreds of thousands of dollars just trying to stay afloat and claw my way back.

So, you will be surprised to hear me say that this may have been the best thing that ever happened to me. It gave me clarity. When everything was stripped away, what really, really mattered? Not what I had achieved, or acquired, and certainly not how I looked, but who I WAS—my character, my spirit. I compare my burns to a forest fire. Whenever there is a forest fire, from the charred remains comes new growth. As holocaust survivor and author Viktor Frankl noted, "What is to give light must also endure burning." My light shined brighter because of the burns.

I had the epiphany that for the first half of our lives we are focused on going to college, having a career, getting married, having children. We have something to aim for. But much like Olympic swimmer Michael Phelps—who suffered from depression and contemplated suicide after collecting a cadre of gold medals—after we achieve those things, we must find another way to find meaning in our lives.

A good friend said to me, "If you aim at nothing, you will hit it every time." After I had achieved my early life goals, there were so many options. *It was the very plethora of choices that made me feel aimless.* What then? As Steven Covey suggests in *The 7 Habits of Highly Effective People*, "Begin with the end in mind." Taking this advice to heart, I wrote my vision of the truest, most beautiful life that I could imagine. I reread it every day. I use this question as a guide: *will taking this action move me closer to that vision?* It gives me clarity and direction. Something to aim for.

I also realized that the first half of our lives is about accomplishing goals, and the second half of our lives is about meaning and purpose. I reread Deepak Chopra's *The Seven Spiritual Laws of Success*. Chopra teaches, "There is something that you can do better than anyone else in the whole world—and for every unique talent and unique expression of that talent, there are also unique needs. When these needs are matched with the creative expression of your talent, that is the spark that creates affluence...When you combine the ability to express your unique talent with service to humanity, then you [find your purpose]."

My purpose is to lift others up. My gift is my ability to use my words and actions to propel others to greatness. My gift of intuition helps me to quickly identify the greatness in others, reveal it to them, and guide them to utilize their gifts. I have the gifts of problem-solving, creativity, and innovation. These gifts help me to guide people out of self-limiting beliefs and perceived obstacles. These gifts were honed while wading through the shit of life. If I had not gone through trauma and difficulties in life, I never would have received these gifts. Understanding that, I approach adversity with gratitude, knowing that opportunities and gifts will reveal themselves.

CHAPTER NINETEEN

BLOOMING

*"And the day came when the risk to remain tight
in a bud was more painful than the
risk it took to blossom."*

—ANAÏS NIN

The day came that I could no longer live in the shadows. It was time to step fully into the light. When COVID hit, I realized that there were no guarantees in life. Life is not a dress rehearsal. We only have one life to live. It was time to share my story because who knows how much longer I have on this planet?

For much of my life, it was a struggle just to survive, to hold it together, to stay above water. I began to thrive when I changed my mindset. I found the gifts in my stories. Instead of controlling me, these painful memories *serve me now*. They serve as reminders of who I am, my strengths, the lessons learned, and wisdom earned.

These gifts are the nutrients that I need to grow. By surrounding myself with my "circle of light"—the friends who support me—I regularly receive the "water" that I need. This circle also delicately prunes me by providing constructive criticism. By removing the toxic people from my life, I have set boundaries—much like a fence around a garden to keep rodents out. These boundaries are critical to thriving; no one gets to dive-bomb in and destroy my growth.

I've learned to surrender and embrace this journey called life. I choose to approach life through a lens of discovery, empathy, compassion, forgiveness, adventure, and humor. In that spirit, I have a wonderful relationship with my ex-husband, Jason. He is a great father and my boys have a strong relationship with him. My sister has become my best friend. I genuinely cherish our relationship. I have compassion for my friends who were horrible to me—all of us are flawed and behave badly on occasion. Many of those relationships have been healed. Others aren't allowed inside the fence. I'm a work in progress, but at age fifty-three, I'm just beginning to bloom. Watch out, world! I'm excited to see what life has in store for me.

ACKNOWLEDGMENTS

Thank you to the friends who have supported me through this journey called life. I am especially grateful to Stephanie Engnes, who has always shown up and supported me. Thank you to Dr. Jill Grimes for having faith in me and encouraging me to write. Your words of encouragement stayed with me through this process. Thank you to Dr. Sherry Dickey for shepherding me through the painful process of facing my past and healing those wounds. Thank you to Deb Gabor for inspiring me and encouraging me. Thank you to Mark Halsell for calling me on my shit, holding space open for me to be completely vulnerable, and offering words of encouragement. Thank you to Amber Davis for always showing up—whether to hold my hair when I was sick or to help me with my fashion decisions. Thank you to Jenny Burnley. I am incredibly grateful for your expertise and kindness. I wouldn't be able to face the world today if it weren't for you. Thank you to Dr. Marcelo Antunes for restoring my face and my spirit, and holding my hand through the process. Finally, thank you to my sister, Tiffany Hunter; I am so grateful for our relationship. Together, we cried and laughed as we explored our past, unearthing memories. Thank you for supporting me through this book-writing process and through life.

APPENDIX

Michael Lee Bourland's Personal Mission Statement

I do what is right.
I don't do what is wrong.

My most basic values are those of honesty,
fairness and trustworthiness.

I believe in forgiving the mistakes of others
while quickly admitting my own.

As a Husband, I know that Cindy is the most important
other person in my life. It is important to me that
I give her my constant support and love.

As a Son and a Brother, I am loving and unselfish.
Mom, Dad and Greg were my first family and their happiness
and success is very important to me. It is important
to me to nurture my relationship with them.

I am a good Friend. It is important for me to be "there"
for my friends when they need me to be.

As a Professional, I am productive and disciplined.
I focus on becoming successful and achieving my goals.
It gives me great pleasure to help others
become successful.

I value the strength of my intellect as well as my body.
I exercise both regularly.

I am efficient in my use of time without
subordinating people to schedules. I know that people
and relationships are more important than
keeping to a timetable.

I concentrate all my abilities and efforts on the
task at hand. I am results-oriented.

I defend those who are absent.

It is important to me to be financially successful.

I am centered in my principles.
I have the will and the integrity to subordinate my feelings,
my impulses and my moods to those principles.

This Mission Statement is my constitution,
my changeless core, the solid expression of my
vision and values. It is the criterion by which
I measure everything else in my life.

BOOK GROUP QUESTIONS

1. Discuss a defining moment in your life. How did that moment define you?

2. Discuss a terrible event that turned out to be a blessing.

3. What was your favorite part of the book?

4. Who in your life frustrated you or hurt you the most? In what ways can you forgive them? How can you set better boundaries with them?

5. What are you doing to fit in that is actually making you miserable? How can you change your behavior to live a more authentic life?

6. What are things that you are willing to stand up for, no matter who is watching?

7. Do you have a personal vision statement? What does it or should it include? How does it guide your choices?

8. In what ways has shame shaped your life? How would you live your life differently if you didn't feel ashamed?

9. What are you holding onto for status that is actually hurting you? Are you ready to let it go?

10. Give an example of an area of your life where changing your mindset could change your life. Write a positive affirmation. Read it aloud every day.

Made in the USA
Coppell, TX
16 November 2021

65832033R00134